Responding

TO

Healthcare

Reform

Responding TO Healthcare Reform

A Strategy Guide *for* Healthcare Leaders

Daniel B. McLaughlin

ACHE Management Series

Your board, staff, or clients may also benefit from this book's insight. For more information on quantity discounts, contact the Health Administration Press Marketing Manager at (312) 424-9470.

This publication is intended to provide accurate and authoritative information in regard to the subject matter covered. It is sold, or otherwise provided, with the understanding that the publisher is not engaged in rendering professional services. If professional advice or other expert assistance is required, the services of a competent professional should be sought.

The statements and opinions contained in this book are strictly those of the authors and do not represent the official positions of the American College of Healthcare Executives or the Foundation of the American College of Healthcare Executives.

15   14   13   12   11   5   4   3   2

Library of Congress Cataloging-in-Publication Data

McLaughlin, Daniel B., 1945–
  Responding to healthcare reform : a strategy guide for healthcare
leaders / Daniel B. McLaughlin.
     p.
  Includes bibliographical references and index.
  ISBN 978-1-56793-416-8 (alk. paper)
  1. Health insurance—Law and legislation—Economic aspects—United
States. 2. Health care reform—Economic aspects—United States. I.
Title.
  [DNLM: 1. United States. Patient Protection and Affordable Care
Act. 2. Insurance, Health—economics—United States. 3. Insurance,
Health—legislation & jurisprudence—United States. 4. Guideline
Adherence—United States. 5. Health Care Reform—economics—United
States. 6. Health Care Reform—legislation & jurisprudence—United
States. W 32.5 AA1]
  KF1183.M35 2011
  344.7303'210425—dc22   2010054502

The paper used in this publication meets the minimum requirements of American National Standard for Information Sciences—Permanence of Paper for Printed Library Materials, ANSI Z39.48-1984.♾ ™

Acquisitions editor: Janet Davis; Project manager: Helen-Joy Lynerd; Cover designer: Marisa Jackson; Layout: Putman Productions LLC

Found an error or a typo? We want to know! Please e-mail it to hap1@ache.org, and put "Book Error" in the subject line.

For photocopying and copyright information, please contact Copyright Clearance Center at www.copyright.com or at (978) 750-8400.

Health Administration Press
A division of the Foundation of the American
    College of Healthcare Executives
One North Franklin Street, Suite 1700
Chicago, IL 60606-3529
(312) 424-2800

To my wife, Sharon, and daughters, Kelly and Katie

Contents

Foreword

THE AFFORDABLE CARE Act of 2010 (ACA) is historic, comprehensive, and bipartisan. Given the talk about death panels, socialized medicine, tea parties, and solid Republican opposition, you may find this hard to believe. Since my election to the US Senate in 1978 and my selection for membership on the Senate's Finance Committee, I have been engaged in health policy reform—much of the work around changes in Medicare payment policy, and all of it bipartisan. Unfortunately this changed in 1993 and 1994. Nonetheless, the ACA is historic because it is the first time ever that Congress has passed a comprehensive reform of all of US health policy. Much of the language in the ACA is based on the experiences of both Republicans and Democrats in Congress since the Clinton health policy failure.

The goals of the ACA are to create a uniquely American health system by providing consumers with comparative information and the financial motivation to use it; motivate care delivery systems to improve the health of communities with high-value, low-cost services; and rebalance the patient–professional relationship. In the past, national health policy has focused on incremental efforts to reduce the supply of medical services or regulate prices. Comprehensive policy reform allows communities across the country to respond to the challenge of value-based care design and delivery in unique ways and to be rewarded with a share of the savings generated by changed behavior and a healthier population.

My colleague Dan McLaughlin has spent a lifetime in just this kind of professional endeavor. As the administrator of one of the largest hospitals and the largest county health services system in Minnesota, he has an understanding of what health is, what affects it, and the importance of health professional leadership for improvement. As director of the Centers for

Health and Medical Affairs at the Opus College of Business, Mr. McLaughlin teaches systems change and leadership. In this book, *Responding to Healthcare Reform,* he brings to the reader everything that is needed to create local strategies to successfully meet the tidal wave of policy and systems change that will result from the implementation of the ACA.

This book allows the reader to connect the best clinical practices with the best operational practices to enable value-based production of healthcare services. The "great recession of 2008–09" marks the end of more than 50 years of a US economy that could not be sustained forever. The new economy will demand of education, energy, healthcare, and housing what the old economy demanded of more globally competitive industries like manufacturing and finance: value for money, productivity, Six Sigma quality, and safety. Dan McLaughlin's systems approach to strategy creation in the reformed healthcare environment enables the reader to get ahead of the learning curve. This is the only book you need to own to be successful in shaping the future of the predictably unique US health system.

David Durenberger
US Senate, 1978 to 1995

Acknowledgments

THE LEGISLATIVE ARENA can be both challenging and exciting, and I had the opportunity to participate in it as a policy analyst and as the leader of a lobbying team.

Hennepin County is the largest county in Minnesota and surrounds Minneapolis, and I had the opportunity to lobby many legislative proposals in the Minnesota Legislature. I want to thank Hennepin County Commissioners Randy Johnson, Mike Opat, and Peter McLaughlin (not a relative) for their support and education during those years.

I also would like to thank Representatives Lee Greenfield and Tom Huntley of the Minnesota House and Senator Linda Berglin of the Minnesota Senate for their support of Hennepin County and all of the excellent healthcare legislation they enacted over the past 20 years.

At the federal level I am grateful to former Congressman Martin Sabo of Minnesota for his support and former Senator David Durenberger of Minnesota. David is a gift to Minnesota, where he continues to teach students at the University of St. Thomas and directs the National Institute of Health Policy.

At the University of St. Thomas I am indebted to Dean Chris Puto and Associate Dean Michael Garrison of the Opus College of Business for their support of my center and work. I also am supported by faculty colleagues Professors John Militello and Mick Sheppeck, with whom I have ongoing discussions and debates about the role of strategy in healthcare. I also want to thank Erica Lyons of the Center for Health and Medical Affairs and Jeff Snegosky, who assisted in research for the companion website.

This is the third book I have written for Health Administration Press, and without their excellent staff support it would not have been possible.

Thanks once again to Janet Davis, acquisitions director; Kaye Muench, marketing director; Ed Avis, editorial director; and Helen-Joy Lynerd, project manager.

Finally I want to thank the United States Congress and President Obama for this new significant improvement in American health policy. Although both parties did not agree on the final product, the hard and courageous work of these elected officials has moved this nation's healthcare system into a new era.

—Dan McLaughlin

Preface

I HAVE ALWAYS enjoyed health policy—as a student, teacher, and participant. For most of my career I worked for Hennepin County, which surrounds Minneapolis, Minnesota. I spent 30 years as an administrator in the
Hennepin County Medical Center and the last 8 as its CEO. I also initiated and led the Hennepin County Health Policy Center, which drafted
and lobbied legislation to support the healthcare system of the county. The
practical application of health policy can be frustrating but is essential to
the success of a county-based health system.

I also had the opportunity to work on the Clinton Healthcare Reform
bill in 1992 and 1993 as a representative of the National Association of
Counties. The federal process is essentially the same as that at the state
level—but a lot more intense because of larger stakes.

Because of my experience in helping to craft health policy, the past two
years of debate and the final enactment of the Patient Protection and
Affordable Care Act (PPACA—now shortened to the Affordable Care
Act or the ACA) were intensely interesting to me. The committee hearings
on C-SPAN were fascinating to watch as various stakeholders maneuvered
to ensure that their concepts were included in the final bill.

Most of the press coverage of the legislative process was related to the
politics of health reform, with little practical discussion or analysis of the
details of many of the bill's provisions. Understanding and applying the final bill can be difficult, as is knowing what strategies to pursue to comply
with the ACA—hence this book.

Legislation arises from a strongly perceived need and is drafted by experts. These experts come from

- government agencies,
- trade associations,
- professional societies,
- academics,
- think tanks (usually Washington, DC–based), and
- legislative committee staff.

The legislation can seem disjointed and complex because of these multiple inputs to the process. More importantly, the legislation is unclear about what new strategies need to be implemented or old strategies abandoned. The ACA is unusually confusing because the final bill never went to conference committee where much of the logic of a bill is set.

Numerous resources clarifying the details of the law are available from consulting firms, trade associations, and advocacy groups. In some cases these resources will be sufficient to make adjustment in operations and strategy.

However, this book provides an additional and higher-level strategic option as a neutral and academically based resource to assist the healthcare leader in crafting and revising strategic plans.

Parts 1, 2, and 3 of the book focus on the three underlying theories of the ACA:

- Taking a systems approach to change
- Using financial incentives for change
- Supporting market competition for change

Although complex, the elements of the ACA are constructed in an interrelated manner to achieve the goals of increased access to care, improved quality, and decreased growth in cost. For healthcare CEOs, this type of theoretical understanding is critical to creating strategy that will succeed in a new environment and that fits well with the organization's capabilities and culture.

My research explains the underlying basis for those sections of the ACA that are critical to strategy formulation. Most sections are based on demonstrations, pilots, and controlled trials. I encourage healthcare executives (and/or their staff colleagues) to explore the references in depth and in some cases visit some of the organizations that have superior results. The companion website for this book (ache.org/books/reform) is updated frequently, and as new research findings become available they will be posted there.

Another tool used to develop strategy in an uncertain environment is multiple scenario analysis. By creating scenarios that are unique but based on possible future events, an organization can test its strategies to ascertain its robustness under various conditions. This book contains 20 such scenarios, and I invite the reader to create more. Appendix A contains a list of discussion questions that can be helpful to foster the creation of new scenarios.

Finally, Part 4 discusses the future, as no health policy is ever static—legislation is modified every year. I frequently encounter a few inspired students who want to "do policy." As most of the readers of this book will not run for office, I provide practical suggestions on how to participate in the crafting and enactment of new legislation or make refinements to the ACA.

The ACA is one of the most significant changes to American health policy since the advent of Medicare and Medicaid. Its success is in the hands of today's healthcare leaders. I wish you well.

—Dan McLaughlin

Introduction

TIDAL WAVES ARE difficult to see until they crash onto the beach. The Affordable Care Act[1] of 2010 contains a tidal wave of changes to the US healthcare system—many of which are not yet apparent but which will forever change the delivery of care in the United States. Those leaders who assume the system will not change dramatically will struggle as the wave of changes grows in intensity. Successful healthcare leaders will anticipate this new environment and devise effective strategies to use these changes to significantly benefit their organization.

This book provides a foundation for creating successful strategies in the newly reformed healthcare environment. The contours of healthcare's future will clearly be shaped by the Affordable Care Act (ACA). Because the ACA contains over 400 complex sections, a straightforward reading of it is of limited use in strategy creation. However, an understanding of the underlying theories that shaped the ACA can be useful in anticipating the future environment of US healthcare.

This book is organized around the three fundamental theories of the ACA. Through these theoretical viewpoints a more complete understanding of the framework for the policy changes that were eventually included in the law can be obtained:

- Systems—how does each element in the system interact with and affect the other elements to achieve the desired outcomes (patient health)?
- Funds flow and incentives—how can revenue and payment systems be designed to create change in behaviors to achieve desired outcomes (increased quality and patient satisfaction with lowered cost)?

- Markets—how can markets be made to operate effectively to allow the "invisible hand" of capitalism to achieve the desired outcomes (provider market share and profit)?

Each of the three parts includes chapters that focus on key sections of the bill that are in alignment with the theory.[2] The Systems Section addresses

- chronic disease management and primary care,
- quality and efficiency, and
- prevention.

The Funds Flow Section reviews

- incentives that reward wanted provider behavior,
- policies that discourage unwanted provider behavior and fraud,
- backup policies should incentives fail, and
- opportunities in the safety net.

The Markets Section addresses

- universal coverage and health insurance exchanges, and
- the role of government in maintaining a competitive marketplace.

Each section ends with multiple scenario analysis and strategic options for the policies. The book concludes with a chapter about the future and the health leader's role in shaping it.

THE GROUNDWORK IS LAID

Considering the debate on health reform in 2009 and 2010 might lead one to conclude that the final product is simply a random collection of ideas from various interest groups, academics, and politicians. However, the ACA is the result of many years of health policy research, demonstration projects, pilots, and many of the best practices being used by leading healthcare organizations throughout the country.

Senator Max Baucus (chair of the Senate Finance Committee) released a comprehensive report on November 12, 2008, just eight days after the presidential election. "Call to Action: Health Reform 2009" (Baucus 2008) includes many of the features and architecture of the final law. This report was well researched and included over 290 footnotes from scholarly research

Source	Theory	Exhibit I.1 Source of Theories Contained in the ACA
Academics, nonpartisan think tanks, and career federal officials	Systems	
Liberals	Funds flow and incentives	
Conservatives	Markets	

publications and reports on the results of many federally funded pilot projects and demonstrations. It outlined the key elements needed for reforming the US health system:

- Increased access to affordable healthcare
- Improved value by reforming the healthcare delivery system
- Financing changes for a more efficient system

Although the enactment of the ACA was clearly partisan, it includes many policies that have been recommended over the years by Republicans and Democrats. In addition, many of the policies were advanced by non-partisan academics and career federal staff. Although generalization is always dangerous, the source of specific policies can be grouped as shown in Exhibit I.1.

THE THREE THEORIES

Systems View

A useful systems view of US healthcare starts with the patient–provider relationship. This is the "system" that is the most visible to patients and providers. The provider is frequently a physician but includes healthcare professionals such as nurses, pharmacists, chiropractors, and others.

Both the provider and the patient are influenced by other systems, and Exhibit I.2 illustrates this relationship.

The providers deliver the service based on the diagnostic and therapeutic tools available. The patients receive the service in the context of their own behaviors (e.g., smoking, weight control) and the burden of illness they may bear as a result of genetic makeup, their living and working environments, and other factors beyond their control.

This model can be expanded outward by examining the details of each element (Exhibit I.3).

Exhibit I.2 Core Elements of the US Healthcare System

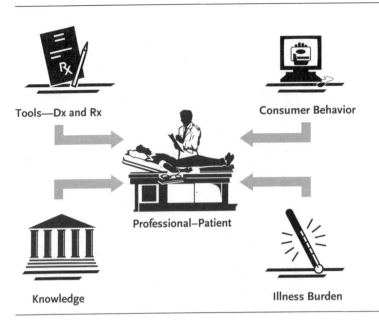

Tools—Dx and Rx

Consumer Behavior

Professional–Patient

Knowledge

Illness Burden

Exhibit I.3 Second-Level Model of the US Healthcare System

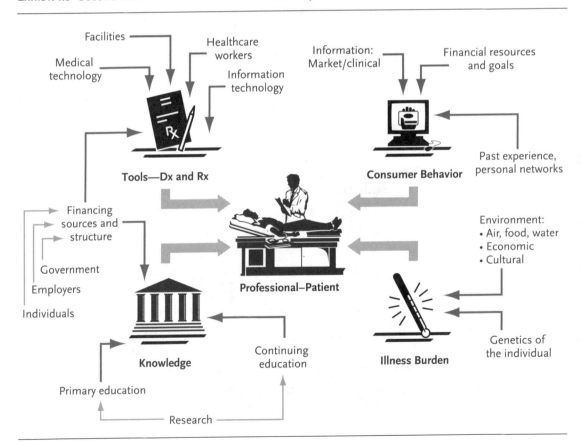

Facilities

Medical technology

Healthcare workers

Information technology

Information: Market/clinical

Financial resources and goals

Tools—Dx and Rx

Consumer Behavior

Past experience, personal networks

Financing sources and structure

Government

Employers

Individuals

Professional–Patient

Environment:
• Air, food, water
• Economic
• Cultural

Knowledge

Continuing education

Illness Burden

Genetics of the individual

Primary education

Research

This expanded model has many interlocking elements. For example, the provider has an array of tools that are used for diagnosis and treatment: medical technology, facilities (hospitals, clinics, etc.), healthcare professionals, and, most recently, advanced healthcare information technology. The use of these tools is affected by financing structures (see the incentives and funds flow model in the next section.)

Knowledge is another key to the effective functioning of the system. The system starts with basic research, the research is translated into practice, and then this knowledge is conveyed to practitioners through formal and informal education.

The consumers' behavior is affected by the information they gather (much of it now from the Internet), the financial constraints and incentives of their health insurance, and the information they acquire from their family, friends, and coworkers.

The final aspect of the systems view of healthcare is the underlying environmental factors that influence an individual's health, such as genetic makeup.

The authors of the ACA sought to improve the US healthcare system by improving almost all of the elements in the system. For example, the need for improvements in the workforce—particularly in primary care—was included in Title V: "Health Care Workforce." Healthy communities affect the disease burden on individuals, and this is addressed in the ACA in §4201, "Community Transformation Grants." The need for ongoing and comprehensive research on the effectiveness of various treatments is addressed in §6301-6302, "Patient Centered Outcomes Research."

Finally, Crosson and Tollen (2010) demonstrated that large integrated systems can deliver high-quality care cost effectively. These systems effectively manage, align, and optimize most of the elements shown in Exhibit I.3. The designers of the ACA included many elements to encourage the growth of integrated systems.

Funds Flow and Incentives View

"It's not about the money—it's about the money." This quote from a leading health plan CEO provides a concise summary of the confusing financial signals currently inherent in the US healthcare system.

For example, most of the hospitals in the United States are religious and charitable institutions and maintain a nonprofit legal status, yet many of these institutions compete as aggressively as any global public for-profit company. Physicians uniformly attempt to provide optimal care but are

Exhibit I.4
Balancing
Payment
Incentives
in the ACA

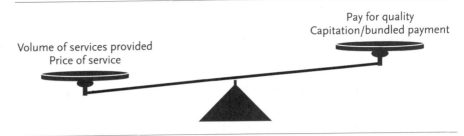

Pay for quality
Capitation/bundled payment

Volume of services provided
Price of service

Exhibit I.5
Balancing
the Newly
Insured with
Reductions
in the Increase
in Medicare
Payments

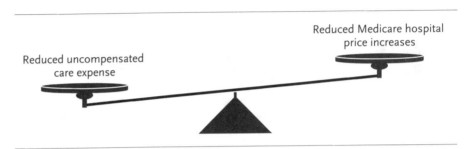

Reduced Medicare hospital
price increases

Reduced uncompensated
care expense

clearly influenced by fee schedules and financial incentives to provide services that may be of limited value.

The designers of the ACA understood this historic conflict between organizations' desire to provide quality services and their desire to maximize revenue and profit. Exhibit I.4 demonstrates the incentives dilemma as providers need to balance the existing fee-for-service system—which rewards volume and price—with the new elements of the ACA that reward quality and efficiency. Perhaps the greatest question of reform is whether the new incentives in the ACA are strong enough to tip this scale.

Another funds flow element of the ACA that will have a significant effect on providers is the balance between a significant reduction in uncompensated care and a reduction of Medicare base rate payment increases. Exhibit I.5 provides an illustration of this redirected funds flow.

Funding policies and incentives in the ACA are designed to move care for an individual to its lowest cost site. Exhibit I.6 shows a generic mapping of this movement. For example, individuals who live in healthy communities, live healthy lifestyles, and get regular preventive services are less likely to need the more expensive professional services of doctors and hospitals. Even when clinical services are required, the ACA provides incentives for the use of the lowest cost and most effective service (e.g., home health as opposed to inpatient care).

Policymakers who believe in government-administered pricing and incentives can point to past successes. Medicare has had a relatively positive

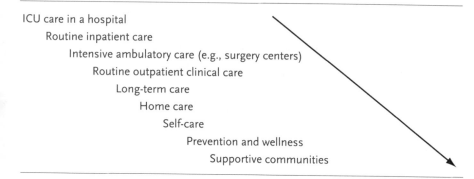

**Exhibit I.6
Incentives
in the ACA
Encourage
Lowest Cost
Site of Care**

ICU care in a hospital
Routine inpatient care
Intensive ambulatory care (e.g., surgery centers)
Routine outpatient clinical care
Long-term care
Home care
Self-care
Prevention and wellness
Supportive communities

record of using administered pricing to meet policy gains. For example, the prospective payment system using diagnosis-related groups (DRGs) that was implemented in 1983 succeeded in reducing hospital length of stay significantly more than was predicted at the time of enactment. The Congressional Budget Office estimated that the DRG system would save Medicare $10 billion from 1983 to 1986. Actual savings were $21 billion (Gabel 2010).

Incentives are the carrot in the toolbox of the policymaker. The stick is regulation. Unfortunately, regulation tends to freeze systems in place and provides limited mechanisms for innovation or needed system change. Therefore, the authors of the ACA chose incentives as their primary policy tool, but if they fail, new regulations will appear. The Independent Payment Advisory Board (§3403) will be the vehicle for this correction to the system.

Markets View

The healthcare system can also be conceptualized as a series of buyers and sellers of products. In this classic view of market-based capitalism, the sellers will be rewarded if their products provide high value at low prices. Although many have argued that markets do not work well in healthcare, the authors of the ACA attempted to maintain this important aspect of the system. A markets viewpoint of traditional employment-based health insurance and private healthcare delivery is illustrated in Exhibit I.7.

In this model the initial buyer in the system is the employer, who purchases health insurance on behalf of employees from a health plan. The employees in turn choose their providers from those available in the health plan's network.

The market is becoming more sophisticated because of the increase in high-deductible insurance plans, and because patients are beginning to pick providers based on cost and perceived quality (Robinson and Ginsburg 2009).

Exhibit I.7
Market
Perspective on
Employment-
Based
Healthcare
System

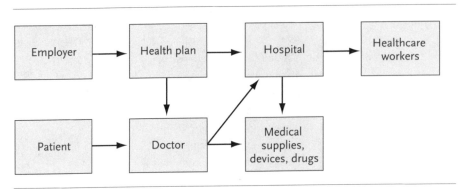

In the markets model, doctors (and other providers) are also buyers as they choose the resources they need to treat the patient. "Resources" include everything from medical supplies to which hospital to use for a particular patient. Hospitals also purchase from other markets for their workforce and supplies. Since health plans pay for most of these items, buying and selling in this market is complex. The general economic theory of market capitalism predicts that the interactions of all of these markets should produce the greatest value at the lowest cost. The characteristics of perfect market competition are (Henderson 2002)

- many buyers and sellers,
- a standardized product,
- mobile resources, and
- buyers with access to complete and comprehensive information.

To reinforce this concept of market competition the ACA has many competitive features, the most prominent of which are the health insurance exchanges (§1311–1313). Instead of direct regulation of health insurance rates (as is done in some European countries) the designers of ACA expect that competition between health plans will contain costs and increase value. The law contains numerous sections in Title I: "Quality, Affordable Health Care for All Americans" that are designed to ensure a fair competitive playing field for health plans and affordability for individuals and small employers.

For health plans to be price competitive they must buy carefully from their suppliers (i.e., doctors, hospitals, pharmaceutical companies). This careful purchasing will encourage providers to improve their operations to deliver the highest value possible. The characteristics of perfect competition and the elements of the new health exchanges are compared in Exhibit I.8.

A unique aspect of the US health system is the health savings account (HSA), which provides a direct financial incentive for consumers to pur-

Exhibit 1.8
Perfect Market
Competition
and the ACA

Perfect Competition	Affordable Care Act—Health Exchanges
Many buyers and sellers	Almost all health plans will be available in the exchanges, and 30 million or more individuals and small firms will buy their insurance in this market.
A standardized product	The exchanges will have four different standardized benefit levels and a standardized benefit set.
Mobile resources	Health plans will be able to compete across state lines. Some healthcare organizations will become national players for both the direct provision of care (e.g., Mayo Clinic and Cleveland Clinic) and health insurance (e.g., UnitedHealth, Wellpoint).
Buyers with complete and comprehensive information	Healthcare.gov provides links to comprehensive data on both costs and quality. These resources will expand greatly in the future.

chase carefully in the healthcare market. Although many observers expected that HSAs would be eliminated in the ACA, they were preserved with only minor modifications (§9004). Over 10 million Americans use a form of health savings accounts and their use is predicted to increase (Fronstin 2010).

Other competitive bidding opportunities exist for durable medical equipment suppliers (§6407) and healthcare systems that wish to participate in the national pilot project for bundled inpatient care payments (§3023).

Relying entirely on market forces to constrain costs in the US health system has not proved effective. However, market competition is an underlying philosophy and important part of the law. If market forces fail to restrain healthcare inflation after the full enactment of the ACA, the next round of legislative action will include much stronger direct federal regulation of all of the financial aspects of the system.

STRATEGY DEVELOPMENT WITH SCENARIO PLANNING

Scenario planning improves an organization's strategic plan and tests its robustness (ability to respond effectively to unexpected environmental changes). Scenario planning is particularly useful in the new, uncertain environment created by the ACA. The model described here is based on the work of Mats Lindgren and Hans Bandhold (2009).

Exhibit I.9
Scenario Cross

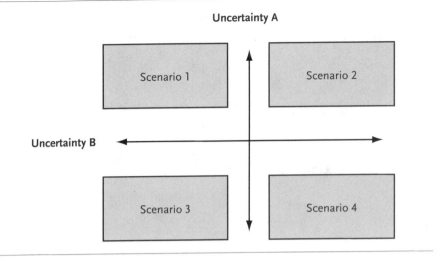

The basic goals of scenario planning are

- a focus on minimizing the risks of maintaining "business as usual,"
- evaluations of new business opportunities and paradigm shifts,
- support and energy for new business concepts and developments, and
- robust plans that respond effectively to unexpected environmental changes.

The first step in creating scenarios is to identify significant trends that will affect the organization during the time horizon in the strategic plan. The trends that are used to develop possible scenarios in chapters 4, 7, and 9 are based on key policies contained in the ACA. Once these key policies have been identified, they can be ranked on importance to the success of reform and also on uncertainty. The trends with the highest uncertainty and importance are then arrayed in a scenario cross (Exhibit I.9) where the extreme outcomes of each policy are displayed.

Four different scenarios emerge from these intersections. Good scenario planning practice suggests that each scenario have a memorable title and a short descriptive paragraph. For example, one policy goal of the ACA is to improve chronic disease management through the "meaningful use" of information technology. This may work well or be ineffective depending on the ability of an organization to successfully install the new complex systems. Another goal of the ACA is to increase the supply of primary care physicians. Although most policy analysts agree that an increased primary care workforce is necessary for reform to succeed, the lower salaries earned by primary care physicians may continue to limit the supply of these general practitioners.

Exhibit I.10
Scenario Cross
for Chronic
Disease
Management

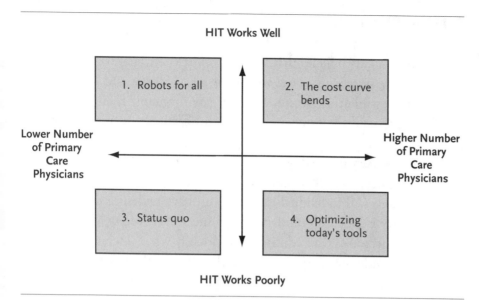

The scenario cross for these two policies is Exhibit I.10, and the strategic implications of these four scenarios are explored in Chapter 4.

The remainder of this book provides a more detailed look into aspects of the ACA that have strategic implications for the healthcare leader. (Only those aspects of the law that bear on strategy options for the healthcare executive are examined.) Each chapter takes important elements of the ACA and explains its relationship to the three theories.

HOW TO USE THIS BOOK

The ACA was originally over 2,400 pages long and is accompanied by the final reconciliation bill, which is 200 pages long. Although numerous summaries are available, considering the specific legislative language is useful. This can be accomplished by opening the bill (available in a link on this book's companion website at ache.org/books/reform). This book contains many references to specific sections of the ACA and they will always be preceded by the section symbol (*signum sectionis*) §.

An important adjunct resource to the book is the companion website (ache.org/books/reform). The companion website is updated frequently and should serve as an ongoing resource for strategy formulation. The website is maintained by the author and other members of his team at the Center for Health and Medical Affairs, University of St. Thomas, Minneapolis, Minnesota.

SUMMARY

The ACA contains policies that will promulgate the largest change in the US healthcare system since the enactment of Medicare and Medicaid. To develop successful strategies in this new environment, healthcare leaders should understand the three theories that underlie the numerous policies in the ACA.

The first theory is based on a systems perspective. This theory advances the concept that since all elements of the healthcare system are connected, strategic changes to individual elements can have widespread effects. The second theory is based on funds flow and incentives. Many Medicare programs have succeeded with administered pricing, which includes incentives to change provider behavior. Because of this history, these types of tools are also part of the ACA. Finally, US capitalism and a markets view of the healthcare industry is also a part of the ACA—most prominently on display in the health insurance exchanges, which will be operational in 2014.

Because the interactions of all of the policies contained in the ACA create an uncertain future, scenario planning is a useful tool to test strategy options. This book contains an explanation of elements of the ACA that are important to strategy development along with multiple scenarios for the newly reformed healthcare environment.

NOTES

1. The Affordable Care Act was enacted in March 2010. The law was enacted in two parts: The Patient Protection and Affordable Care Act was signed into law on March 23, 2010, and was amended by the Health Care and Education Reconciliation Act on March 30, 2010. The name "Affordable Care Act" is used to refer to the final, amended version of the law (from www.healthcare.gov/glossary/a/affordable_care.html).

2. Because the ACA is long and complex, only those sections that affect broad strategy decisions are included as part of this analysis. Examples of items not included are responsibilities of employers and individuals to provide insurance, policies for specific segments of care delivery (e.g., cancer hospitals, trauma care, Indian Health Service), technical payment adjustments, workforce enhancements, tax policy, and transparency.

REFERENCES

Baucus, M. 2008. "Call to Action: Health Reform 2009." US Senate Finance Committee, Nov. 12.

Crosson, F. J., and L. A. Tollen. 2010. *Partners in Health: How Physicians and Hospitals Can Be Accountable Together*. San Francisco: Jossey-Bass.

Fronstin, P. 2010. "Health Savings Accounts and Health Reimbursement Arrangements: Assets, Account Balances, and Rollovers, 2006–2009." EBRI Issue Brief, 343.

Gabel, J. R. 2010. "Does the Congressional Budget Office Underestimate Savings from Reform? A Review of the Historical Record." Commonwealth Fund Issue Brief.

Henderson, J. W. 2002. "Health Economics and Policy." Southwestern, page 51.

Lindgren, M., and H. Bandhold. 2009. *Scenario Planning: The Link between Future and Strategy*. New York: Palgrave-Macmillan.

Robinson, J. C., and P. B. Ginsburg. 2009. "Consumer-Driven Health Care: Promise and Performance." [Online information; retrieved 2/28/09.] http://content.healthaffairs.org/content/28/2/w272.full?sid=059645fd-0679-4b3c-8df8-2b25e1571360

ADDITIONAL ONLINE RESOURCES

The Complete Patient Protections and Affordable Care Act

The Department of Health and Human Services (HHS) maintains the complete law on its website. It is likely that HHS will update this as Congress amends the law. The complete Patient Protection and Affordable Care Act can be found at http://docs.house.gov/energycommerce/ppacacon.pdf with an HHS summary here: www.healthcare.gov/law/provisions/index.html

Congressional Research Service (CRS) Summary of the Law

A major role of the CRS is to summarize important and major legislation. This complete and detailed summary is available at the back of this book and at the following: http://thomas.loc.gov/cgi-bin/bdquery/z?d111:HR03590:@D&summ2=m&

Kaiser Summary of the Law

This 13-page document summarizes all the major provisions contained in the ACA. www.kff.org/healthreform/upload/8061.pdf

Kaiser Health Insurance Cost Calculator

This website allows the user to calculate the projected cost of health insurance in 2014. This estimate includes the subsidy amount, which is based on the enrollee's income. http://healthreform.kff.org/subsidycalculator.aspx

Current Updates on the ACA from Kaiser

http://healthreform.kff.org/

For additional and more current references and resources please check the companion website at ache.org/books/reform.

PART 1

Systems

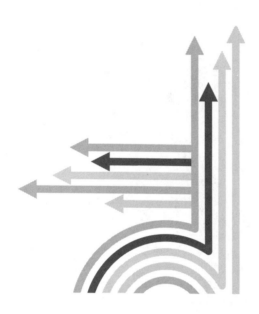

CHAPTER 1

Chronic Disease Management and Primary Care

THE FIRST UNDERLYING theory of the ACA is the use of systems analysis to change how each element in the system interacts with other elements to achieve the desired outcomes. The systems approach is used to promote one of the most significant changes to the American healthcare system—the improvement of the care for those with chronic disease.

The ACA contains a number of policy initiatives that focus on improving care for these patients. Chronic care comes with a high cost and high variability in treatment. Knowledge on best practices in chronic disease management has accumulated over the past 30 years, and the ACA contains many new policies that promote the application of this knowledge throughout the provider community.

Exhibit 1.1 illustrates the distribution of costs associated with the care of patients with chronic diseazses. Note the high cost for people with three or more chronic conditions (89 percent). In addition, the costs of chronic disease care vary greatly throughout the country (Exhibit 1.2).

THE CHRONIC CARE MODEL

Dr. Edward Wagner of the MacColl Institute for Healthcare Innovation, a leader in the improvement of chronic care, has developed one of the most widely accepted models for chronic disease management. The first important element of Wagner's model is population-based outreach, which ensures that all patients in need of chronic disease management receive it. Next, treatment plans are created that are sensitive to each patient's preferences. The most current evidence-based medicine is employed—this process is

Exhibit 1.1 Medicare Spending for Chronic Conditions	

Exhibit 1.1
Medicare
Spending
for Chronic
Conditions

Two-Thirds of Medicare Spending Is for People with Five or More Chronic Conditions

No chronic conditions, 1%

1–2 chronic conditions, 10%

5 or more chronic conditions, 66%

3 chronic conditions, 10%

4 chronic conditions, 13%

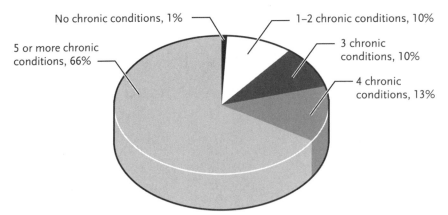

Source: The Commonwealth Fund; data from G. Anderson and J. Horvath, *Chronic Conditions: Making the Case for Ongoing Care* (Baltimore, Md.: Partnership for Solutions, Dec. 2002). Used with permission.

Exhibit 1.2 Costs of Care for Medicare Beneficiaries with Multiple Chronic Conditions

			Average Annual Reimbursement				Ratio of Percentile Groups	
		Average	10th Percentile	25th Percentile	75th Percentile	90th Percentile	90th to 10th	75th to 25th
All 3 Conditions	2001	$31,792	$20,960	$23,973	$37,879	$43,973	2.10	1.58
	2005	$38,004	$25,732	$29,936	$44,216	$53,019	2.06	1.48
Diabetes + Heart Failure	2001	$18,461	$12,747	$14,355	$20,592	$27,310	2.14	1.43
	2005	$23,056	$16,144	$18,649	$26,035	$32,199	1.99	1.40
Diabetes + COPD	2001	$13,188	$8,872	$10,304	$15,246	$18,024	2.03	1.48
	2005	$15,367	$11,317	$12,665	$17,180	$20,062	1.77	1.36
Heart Failure + COPD	2001	$22,415	$15,355	$17,312	$25,023	$32,732	2.13	1.45
	2004	$27,498	$19,787	$22,044	$31,709	$37,405	1.89	1.44

COPD = chronic obstructive pulmonary disease.

Source: Commonwealth Fund National Scorecard on U.S. Health System Performance, 2008. Data from G. Anderson and R. Herbert, Johns Hopkins University analysis of Medicare Standard Analytical Files (SAF) 5% Inpatient Data. Used with permission.

aided by clinical information systems with built-in decision support. The patient is encouraged to change risky behaviors and to manage himself better. The actual clinical visit changes in the Wagner model to allow more time for interaction between physicians and patients with complicated clinical issues. Visits for routine or specialized matters are delivered by other health-care professionals (e.g., nurses, pharmacists, dieticians, lay health workers). Close follow-up supported by clinical information system registries and patient reminders is also characteristic of effective chronic disease management (Improving Chronic Illness Care 2010; Wagner 2000).

THE HITECH ACT AND MEANINGFUL USE

Chronic disease management is information intensive and information dependent. The American Recovery and Reinvestment Act of 2009 (ARRA) includes the Health Information Technology for Economic and Clinical Health Act (HITECH Act), which established programs under Medicare and Medicaid to provide incentive payments for the "meaningful use" of certified electronic health records (EHR) technology.

The goals of the HITECH legislation are to improve healthcare outcomes, facilitate access to care, and simplify care. These goals are particularly important to patients with chronic disease. As regulations were contemplated for the payment of incentives for the installation of health information technology, two perspectives were apparent. Many vendors felt that technical specifications and requirements should be used to certify these new systems for federal incentive payments. However, many clinicians with experience in informatics felt that this new government incentive should only be paid if the EHR systems were used in a meaningful manner to improve patient care. This latter view prevailed. Therefore, the goals of HITECH will be met when the EHR is used in a meaningful way.

Three components of Stage I Meaningful Use have been identified:

1. Use of a certified EHR in a meaningful manner such as e-prescribing
2. Use of certified EHR technology for the exchange of health information (exchange data with other providers of care or business partners such as labs or pharmacies)
3. Use of certified EHR technology to submit clinical quality and other measures to the Department of Health and Human Services (HHS)

Thus, the first stage of meaningful use is capturing and sharing the data. Meaningful Use Stage II involves using the technology in advanced clinical processes, and Stage III involves the meaningful use of an EHR in the context of improved healthcare outcomes. More details on meaningful use are at www.himss.org/ASP/topics_meaningfuluse.asp (HIMSS 2010).

POLICIES TO SUPPORT CHRONIC CARE IN THE ACA

The designers of the ACA included a number of tools that can be used to improve the quality of care for patients with chronic disease and for emergency care:

- Comparative effectiveness research
- Healthcare homes
- Shared decision making

Another ACA tool for improved chronic care is the accountable care organization (ACO); because the ACO is more of a financial incentives–based tool it is addressed in Chapter 5.

The system elements of comparative effectiveness and healthcare home can be located clearly on the healthcare systems map (Exhibit 1.3).

Comparative Effectiveness

The "product line" of American healthcare is immense. The ICD-9[1] contains a multitude of codes—currently over 13,600 diagnosis codes and 3,700 procedure codes. ICD-10 will increase the number of codes significantly. In this mix of tools for diagnosis and treatment, many common clinical approaches have never been adequately tested as to their efficacy.

To address this problem, the ACA and the ARRA established and fund a nonprofit corporation called the Patient-Centered Outcomes Research Institute (ACA §§6301, 6302):

> The purpose of the Institute is to assist patients, clinicians, purchasers, and policymakers in making informed health decisions by advancing the quality and relevance of evidence concerning the manner in which diseases, disorders, and other health conditions can effectively and appropriately be prevented, diagnosed, treated, monitored, and managed through research and evidence synthesis that considers variations in patient subpopulations, and the dissemination of research findings with respect to the relative health outcomes, clinical effectiveness, and appropriateness of the medical treatments, and services. (from §6301)

Exhibit 1.3 Healthcare Systems Map Highlighting Comparative Effectiveness Research and Healthcare Home

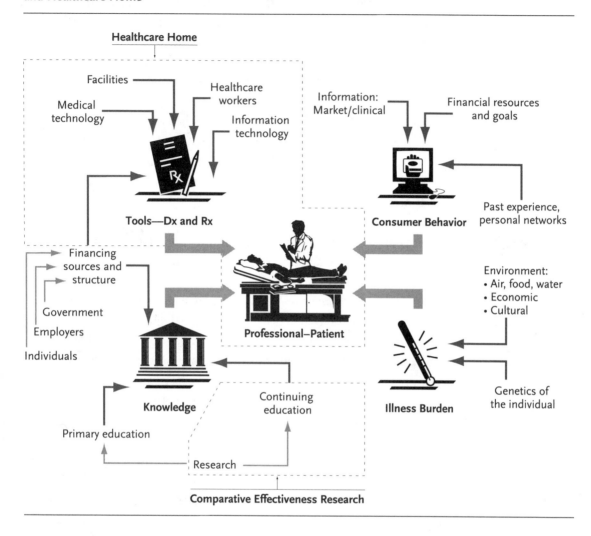

This institute complements the work of the National Institutes of Health and the Agency for Healthcare Research and Quality (AHRQ)—both a part of HHS. One of AHRQ's responsibilities is to assist users to incorporate these research findings into their clinical practice through the use of clinical decision support health information technology.

A major focus for the research topics addressed by the institute is related to chronic disease management.

Healthcare Home

The healthcare home has emerged as an effective tool in the delivery of care to patients with chronic disease. The American Academy of Pediatrics (AAP

COPP 1967) introduced the medical home concept in 1967; it then referred to a central location for archiving a child's medical record. In its 2002 policy statement, the AAP expanded the medical home concept to promote care that is accessible, continuous, comprehensive, family-centered, coordinated, compassionate, and culturally effective. Because this concept now involves many additional types of health professionals it has been renamed the healthcare home.

In 2007, the four major primary care associations (American Academy of Family Physicians [AAFP], American Academy of Pediatrics [AAP], American College of Physicians [ACP], and American Osteopathic Association [AOA]) developed a joint statement on the principles for the patient-centered medical home (AAFP 2010):

- *Personal physician:* each patient has an ongoing relationship with a personal physician trained to provide first contact and continuous and comprehensive care.
- *Physician-directed medical practice:* the personal physician leads a team of individuals at the practice level who collectively take responsibility for the ongoing care of patients.
- *Whole person orientation:* the personal physician is responsible for providing for all the patient's healthcare needs or taking responsibility for appropriately arranging care with other qualified professionals. This includes care for all stages of life and involves acute care; chronic care; preventive services; and end-of-life care.
- *Care is coordinated and/or integrated:* care is coordinated across all elements of the healthcare system (e.g., subspecialty care, hospitals, home health agencies, nursing homes) and the patient's community (e.g., family, public and private community-based services). Care is facilitated by registries, information technology, health information exchange, and other means to ensure that patients get the indicated care when and where they need and want it in a culturally and linguistically appropriate manner.
- *Quality and safety:* quality and safety are hallmarks of the medical home, and evidence-based medicine is emphasized.
- *Enhanced access:* care is facilitated through systems, such as open scheduling and expanded hours, and communication between patients, their personal physicians, and practice staff.
- *Payment:* payment appropriately recognizes the added value provided to patients who have a patient-centered medical home.

A recent study on the effectiveness of healthcare homes found three key components needed for success:

- Individualized and intense caring for patients with chronic illness
- Efficient service provision
- Careful selection of specialists (taking into consideration quality and cost)

By carefully implementing these aspects of care, the healthcare homes studied reduced the total cost of care by 15 percent and improved quality, and providers reported a "less frenetic clinical pace" (Milstein and Gilbertson 2009).

The ACA builds on this framework of care delivery and expands the concept to include teams of practitioners in addition to physicians. Section 2703 provides states with the authority to make payments for healthcare homes through their Medicaid systems. Each state will develop rules and payment systems to support the healthcare home; the joint principles mentioned in the previous bulleted list will likely be the basis for the regulatory framework.

Because primary care is delivered by small-group or solo practitioners in some regions of the United States, §3502 provides for the establishment of community health teams to support healthcare homes. These interdisciplinary teams will "collaborate with local primary care providers and existing State and community based resources to coordinate disease prevention, chronic disease management, transitioning between health care providers and settings and case management for patients, including children, with priority given to those amenable to prevention and with chronic diseases or conditions" (from §3502).

Community Care, which began in North Carolina as a pilot project in 1998, is one of the oldest and largest community health team projects specifically designed to support healthcare home programs. "By focusing on improving chronic illness treatment, Community Care has chalked up some big wins. The program reduced asthma patients' emergency department inpatient admissions by 40% between fiscal year 2003 and 2006 and its diabetes monitoring has also seen notable gains" (from §3502) (Community Care of North Carolina 2011).

Finally, Title V of the ACA has numerous provisions to increase the supply, quality, and distribution of primary care physicians and other health professionals. In addition, §5501 provides for increased Medicare payment for primary care; in 2013 all states must set their Medicaid rates of payment for primary care services at Medicare rates or higher. Whether these policies will increase the supply of these professionals is explored in the scenario analysis in Chapter 4.

Shared Decision Making

Patient engagement is a key feature of successful primary care and chronic disease management. The ACA provides a new tool for patient engagement: §3506 "Program to Facilitate Shared Decision Making." Shared decision making is a concept that effectively empowers patients and reduces unnecessary costs in the system. This section provides funding to create patient educational and decision support materials and to disseminate these aids to providers and patients.

The focus of shared decision making is surgery where no single treatment option is right or wrong; rather, the patient and caregivers consider whether one option or another is right for the patient. For example, among women with early-stage breast cancer, both mastectomy and lumpectomy followed by radiation yield similar mortality benefit. Many women have strong preferences for one or the other, so the quality of care extends beyond the surgeon's technical skills to the decision-making process.

Traditionally, patients have delegated treatment decisions to their physicians: The physician diagnoses the patient's illness and recommends treatment, and then the patient gives informed consent. Policymakers, in turn, have assumed that physicians' decisions reflect medical need and patient demand. However, the remarkable degree of variation in the utilization rates of discretionary surgery raises questions about these assumptions.

For example, Wennberg and colleagues (2007) found that in 2002 and 2003 among the 306 US Hospital Referral Regions (HRRs), the incidence of joint replacement for chronic arthritis of the hip or knee and of surgery for low-back pain varied 5.6-, 4.8-, and 5.9-fold, respectively, from the lowest to the highest region. Wennberg found that the pattern of variation was remarkably stable over time; for most common procedures, variation among regions was highly correlated with the pattern a decade before the study was completed.

Shared decision making is a tool that can be used to address this problem. Highly sophisticated and evidence-based patient decision aids inform the patient of the benefits and risks of a procedure. Trained health professionals counsel patients on use of the decision tools and support the patient's decision. Performance monitoring is also part of a shared decision-making program.

Total system costs can be reduced dramatically through the use of shared decision making. A Cochrane review[2] identified trials of seven conditions commonly treated surgically among the Medicare population: arthritis of the hip and knee; low-back pain from a herniated disc; chest pain (stable angina); enlarged prostate (benign prostatic hypertrophy, or BPH); and early-stage prostate and breast cancers. The review documented that although the decision to have surgery following shared decision making (compared to control groups) varied from study to study, a 21 to 44 percent decline was typical. Patients in shared decision-making arms of the trials were better informed about treatment options and made choices more consistent with their values (Wennberg et al. 2007).

SUMMARY

Chronic disease is an important cost driver in the US healthcare system, and 89 percent of Medicare spending is for people with three or more chronic conditions. Fortunately, a chronic care model has been developed and tested that reduces costs and improves quality for patients with chronic disease.

The ACA (and the ARRA) legislate a number of policies to improve chronic care. The knowledge base for best approaches to the treatment of various chronic diseases increases with comparative effectiveness research. Funding for the acquisition and meaningful use of health information technology to care for chronic patients was included in the HITECH act. An increase in training and payment for primary care providers and the use of the healthcare home is also designed to improve chronic care. Shared decision making is a new tool that improves patient engagement and has been shown to dramatically lower costs in many situations.

NOTES

1. The ICD-9 system is a standardized classification of disease, injuries, and causes of death, by etiology and anatomic localization and codified into a six-digit number.

2. The Cochrane Collaboration, established in 1993, is an international network of people helping healthcare providers, policymakers, patients, and patient advocates make well-informed decisions about human healthcare by preparing, updating, and promoting the accessibility of Cochrane Reviews: over 4,000 evidence-based medicine studies so far, published online in *The Cochrane Libra*.

ANNOTATED REFERENCES

American Academy of Family Physicians (AAFP). 2010. "Joint Principles of a Patient-Centered Medical Home Released by Organizations Representing More Than 300,000 Physicians." [Online press release; retrieved 12/30/10.] www.aafp.org/online/en/home/media/releases/2007/20070305pressrelease0.html

American Academy of Pediatrics Council on Pediatric Practice (AAP COPP). 1967. *Standards of Child Health Care*. Elk Grove Village, IL: AAP.

Community Care of North Carolina. 2011. [Online information; retrieved 1/3/11.] www.communitycarenc.com/

> The Community Care of North Carolina program (formerly known as Access II and III) is building community health networks organized and operated by community physicians, hospitals, health departments, and departments of social services. By establishing regional networks, the program is establishing the local systems that are needed to achieve long-term quality, cost, access, and utilization objectives in the management of care for Medicaid recipients.

Health Information Management Systems Society (HIMSS). 2010. "Meaningful Use Onesource." [Online information; retrieved 12/30/10.] www.himss.org/EconomicStimulus/

> The American Recovery and Reinvestment Act of 2009 (ARRA), included significant Medicare and Medicaid incentive payments to providers and hospitals for the "meaningful use" of certified health IT products. The legislation requires the US Department of Health and Human Services to take regulatory action in several areas, including electronic health record (EHR) incentives for eligible professionals and hospitals (Meaningful Use), standards and certification criteria, an HHS Certification Program, and privacy and security. The Health Information Management Systems Society's website contains extensive documentation of this new federal resource.

Improving Chronic Illness Care. 2010. Website. [Online information; retrieved 12/30/10.] www.improvingchroniccare.org/

> This website, provided by the American Academy of Family Physicians, offers resources and information for practitioners on the implementation of the Chronic Care Model. The site includes an exploration of the elements of the Chronic Care Model (www.improvingchroniccare.org/index.php?p=The_Chronic_Care_Model&s=2); a step-by-step video that walks professionals through the model (www.improvingchroniccare.org/index.php?p=The_Model_Talk&s=27); and a practice assessment tool to gauge how a practice is performing on the six dimensions of the Chronic Care Model (www.improvingchroniccare.org/index.php?p=ACIC_Survey&s=35).

Milstein, A., and E. Gilbertson. 2009. "American Medical Home Runs." *Health Affairs* 28 (5): 1317.

Wagner, E. H. 2000. "The Role of Patient Care Teams in Chronic Disease Management." *BMJ: British Medical Journal* 320 (7234): 569.

Wennberg, J. E., A. M. O'Connor, E. D. Collins, and J. N. Weinstein. 2007. "Extending the P4P Agenda, Part 1: How Medicare Can Improve Patient Decision Making and Reduce Unnecessary Care." *Health Affairs* 26 (6): 1564.

CHAPTER 2

Productivity and Quality

TITLE III OF the ACA, "Improving the Quality and Efficiency of Health Care," contains numerous major policy changes to improve healthcare in the United States. A frequent criticism of the US healthcare system has been the unevenness of the quality and safety in care delivery and the significant differences in the cost of care throughout the country (Wennberg, Berkson, and Rider 2008). The sections in Title III are based on a systems approach to solving these problems.

Exhibit 2.1 shows which portions of the systems view are addressed by these policy changes. These sections in the ACA are intended to connect the knowledge of best clinical practices (evidence-based medicine) and best operational practices (e.g., Lean Six Sigma process improvements) with the tools of clinical care delivery. A healthcare organization that can effectively acquire this knowledge and implement new systems of care will succeed in meeting the policy goals of the ACA.[1]

PRODUCTIVITY

Value-Based Purchasing

The first section of Title III (3001) is the hospital value-based purchasing program; its position is an important message to the healthcare provider community. Medicare is making one of the most significant policy shifts since its inception: changing from paying for the volume of services delivered to paying for quality. This program begins in October 2012 and many detailed regulations will be developed for its full implementation. The outline for this program is contained in §3001 of the ACA.

Exhibit 2.1 Total Health System Model: Productivity and Quality Portion

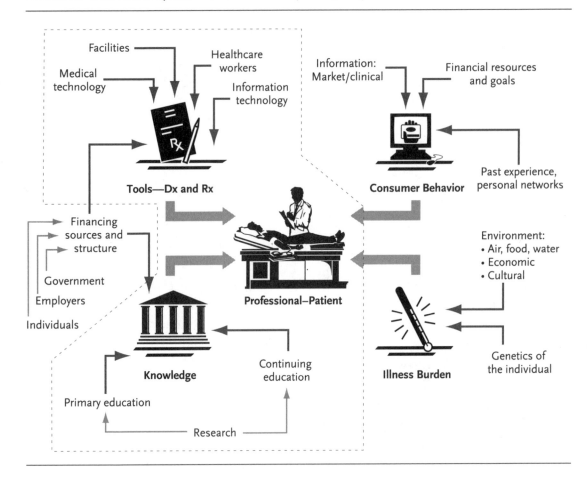

Medicare will reduce hospital value-based purchasing DRG payments by 1 percent in the first year of the program, and this reduction will rise to 2 percent by 2017. The funds Medicare saves through these reductions will be pooled and returned to hospitals that meet clinical quality targets in the areas of

- acute myocardial infarction (AMI),
- heart failure,
- pneumonia,
- surgeries, as measured by the Surgical Care Improvement Project (Quality Net 2011), and
- healthcare-associated infections, as measured by the prevention metrics and targets established in the HHS Action Plan to Prevent Healthcare-Associated Infections (US Department of Health and Human Services 2011).

Medicare will likely expand this list, and the amount of DRG payment linked to quality will rise.

In January 2011 the Centers for Medicare & Medicaid Services (CMS) released a proposed rule to score each hospital on relative achievement and improvement ranges for each applicable measure. A hospital's performance on each quality measure will be evaluated based on the higher of an achievement score in the performance period or an improvement score, which is determined by comparing the hospital's score in the performance period with its score during a baseline period of performance (CMS 2011b).

Physicians are also included in the value-based purchasing approach of Title III. The ACA builds on the existing Physician Quality Reporting Initiative (PQRI) and the Physician Feedback System (CMS 2011a) by adding features in §3002 and §3003. The PQRI provides financial incentives to physicians for reporting quality data to CMS, and the feedback system gives to practitioners reports on the quality of the data they have submitted to CMS. This program is improved in the ACA by an expansion of its scope and integration with the "meaningful use" policies of the HITECH Act (see Chapter 1). In 2013 Medicare will begin to post on a public website information on quality, performance, and patient experience for physicians providing service to Medicare patients (§10331).

In addition, a value-based payment system is outlined in §3007 that is built on the PQRI framework. Although the details are yet to be determined, this section contemplates grouping physician services into an "episode of care" and then making quality payments based on this episode. Rule making for the physician value-based fee schedule will begin in 2013.

Physician services can be measured and rewarded either individually or for a group of doctors. This distinction is important as health policy experts have long argued that a solo physician practice may be too small to effectively measure quality. In addition, system improvements in the delivery of care are much easier to measure at the group level. Therefore, these value purchasing methods have been developed. In fact, §3007 states, "The Secretary shall, as appropriate, apply the payment modifier established under this subsection in a manner that promotes systems-based care."

Productivity Improvements

Section §3401, with its lack of details except for the payment reduction formulas, provides a stark contrast to the detailed treatment of quality improvement in the ACA. This section may be one of the most important aspects of healthcare reform to providers, as it reduces the normal market basket update of Medicare prices by the average business productivity improvement in the United States and specific percentages detailed in the ACA (which range from .25 to .75 percent). Trade associations that represent these providers will likely press Congress to change these formulas over the years, but the policy direction is clear in the ACA. The healthcare system must implement changes to improve its productivity to match the other industries in the United States. McLaughlin and Hays (2008) and Caldwell, Faulker, and Stuenkel (2010) provide an overview of strategies and tools available to providers to improve productivity. Chapters 5 and 6 provide more detail on how the administered pricing systems in Medicare are designed to change provider behavior.

QUALITY

Quality Reporting

The ACA is a health reform bill (not just health insurance reform) and contains significant policies to report on and support the improvement of the quality of healthcare delivery in the United States. Sections §3011 and §3012 call for the development of a national strategy for quality improvement and the coordination of this strategy amongst the many federal and state agencies involved in the healthcare system. The federal agencies are listed in Exhibit 2.2

Section §3013 advances the progress toward quality improvement by providing funding and authority for the continued refinement and construction of quality measures. Section §3014 provides for multi-stakeholder input into the quality improvement process, and §3015 expands the use of these measures for public reporting of quality—much of which is now available on www.healthcare.gov. Because the first sections of Title III outline a value-based purchasing strategy, these quality measures will likely be used as the basis for payment. Quality measures will be developed in the areas of

- health outcomes and functional status of patients;
- the management and coordination of healthcare across episodes of care and care transitions for patients across the continuum of providers, healthcare settings, and health plans;
- the experience, quality, and use of information provided to and used by patients, caregivers, and authorized representatives to inform decision making about treatment options, including the use of shared decision making (see Chapter 1);
- tools and preference-sensitive care (Dartmouth Atlas 2007);
- the meaningful use of health information technology (see Chapter 1);

Exhibit 2.2
Federal Agencies
Involved
in Developing
and Coordinating
a National
Quality
Improvement
Strategy

Department of Health and Human Services	United States Coast Guard
	Federal Bureau of Prisons
Centers for Medicare & Medicaid Services	National Highway Traffic Safety Administration
National Institutes of Health	Federal Trade Commission
Centers for Disease Control and Prevention	Social Security Administration
	Department of Labor
Food and Drug Administration	United States Office of Personnel Management
Health Resources and Services Administration	
Agency for Healthcare Research and Quality	Department of Defense
	Department of Education
Office of the National Coordinator for Health Information Technology	Department of Veterans Affairs
	Veterans Health Administration
Substance Abuse and Mental Health Services Administration	Any other federal agencies and departments with activities relating to improving healthcare quality and safety, as determined by the president
Administration for Children and Families	
Department of Commerce	
Office of Management and Budget	

- the safety, effectiveness, patient-centeredness, appropriateness, and timeliness of care (Institute of Medicine 2001);
- the efficiency of care;
- the equity of health services and health disparities across health disparity populations and geographic areas;
- patient experience and satisfaction;
- the use of innovative strategies and methodologies; and
- other areas determined appropriate by the secretary of HHS.

Health Plans and Medicaid

Because quality reporting for Medicare is currently fairly robust, the ACA extends these policies to health plans and Medicaid. Section §1001/2717 mandates the development and public reporting requirements to

- improve health outcomes through the implementation of activities such as quality reporting, effective case management, care coordination, chronic disease management, and medication and care compliance initiatives;

- implement activities to prevent hospital readmissions through a comprehensive program for hospital discharge that includes patient-centered education and counseling, comprehensive discharge planning, and post-discharge reinforcement by healthcare professionals;
- implement activities to improve patient safety and reduce medical errors through the appropriate use of best clinical practices, evidence-based medicine, and health information technology; and
- implement wellness and health promotion activities.

Section §2701 mandates the creation and reporting of Medicaid quality measures. Because this activity must be done with the states, the process will be slow and complex.

Support for Quality and Productivity Improvement

The Agency for Healthcare Research and Quality (AHRQ) has emerged as one of the key federal agencies to support healthcare reform. Section §3501 gives the agency additional mandates and funding to continue research to

- identify best practices in the delivery of healthcare services;
- find changes in processes of care and systems used by providers that will reliably result in intended health outcomes, improve patient safety and reduce medical errors (such as skill development for healthcare providers in team-based healthcare delivery and rapid cycle process improvement), and facilitate adoption of improved workflow;
- identify healthcare providers, including healthcare systems, single institutions, and individual providers, that
  - deliver consistently high-quality, efficient healthcare services and
  - employ best practices that are adaptable and scalable to diverse healthcare settings or effective in improving care across diverse settings;
- assess research, evidence, and knowledge about what strategies and methodologies are most effective in improving healthcare delivery; and
- determine methods to translate such information rapidly and effectively into practice and to document the sustainability of those improvements.

AHRQ has an excellent website (http://www.ahrq.gov/) that contains the results of studies already undertaken in these areas, and it updates this site frequently. Healthcare organizations that wish to make significant improvements in their operations should fully utilize this exceptional resource.

SUMMARY

Although much of the controversy and press coverage surrounding the enactment of the ACA focused on its health insurance provisions, the ACA also makes significant strides toward improving the quality and efficiency of the US healthcare system.

A new value-based purchasing system will be initiated for Medicare, and Medicare fee-for-service payments will be reduced. Quality reporting will be improved and expanded for physicians, health plans, and Medicaid. A national strategy for quality improvement will be developed and the dissemination of advances in quality and productivity will be increased through the Agency for Healthcare Research and Quality.

NOTE

1. *Make It Happen: Effective Execution in Healthcare Leadership,* by the author, outlines an integrated system to quickly and efficiently implement strategy.

ANNOTATED REFERENCES

Caldwell, C., T. Faulker, and K. Stuenkel. 2010. "Aggressive Cost Reduction: Taking Lean to the Next Level." Presentation at the 2010 Congress on Healthcare Leadership, March 24.
One of the primary tools for productivity improvement is Lean Six Sigma. The presentation by Caldwell and colleagues showed impressive results. The Floyd Medical Center in Northwest Georgia saved $7,599,508 in annual operating costs through the execution of over 650 Lean projects in two-and-a-half years. Caldwell indicated that in his experience as a consultant, savings accrue from reducing these areas of waste:

Waste Type	Improvement Impact
Staffing not matched to demand	41%
Over-inventory/supplies	20%
Materials and information movement	15%
Redundancy/overprocessing	10%
Overcorrection/inspection	6%
Motion	5%
Waiting	1%
Total	100%

Centers for Medicare & Medicaid Services (CMS). 2011a. "Educational Resources." [Online information; retrieved 1/3/11.] www.cms.gov/PQRI/30_EducationalResources.asp

CMS provides both overviews and educational resources for the Physician Quality Reporting System. Eligible professionals are encouraged to contact their professional organizations for additional information and tools that will facilitate participation in the Physician Quality Reporting System.

————. 2011b. "Medicare Program: Hospital Inpatient Value-Based Purchasing Program." [Online proposed rule; published 1/1/3/11.] www.medicarefind.com/searchdetails/ManualData/Attachments/2011-00454_PI.pdf

Dartmouth Atlas. 2007. "Preference-Sensitive Care." A Dartmouth Atlas Project Topic Brief. [Online report; published 1/15/07.] www.dartmouthatlas.org/downloads/reports/preference_sensitive.pdf

Researchers at Dartmouth College have done extensive research in the geographic variation in the provision of "preference-sensitive care." They state:

Preference-sensitive care comprises treatments that involve significant tradeoffs affecting the patient's quality and/or length of life. Decisions about these interventions—whether to have them or not, which ones to have—ought to reflect patients' personal values and preferences, and ought to be made only after patients have enough information to make an informed choice. Sometimes, as with the options for treating early stage breast cancer, the scientific evidence on the main outcome—survival—is quite good; other times, as with treatment options following prostate cancer, the evidence is much weaker.

Institute of Medicine (IOM). 2001. *Crossing the Quality Chasm: A New Health System for the 21st Century.* Washington, DC: National Academies Press.

The Institute of Medicine first addressed these issues in *Crossing the Quality Chasm.* The premise of this landmark study is that there is a chasm between what we know is good medical practice and the way medicine is actually practiced in the United States.

McLaughlin, D., and J. Hays. 2008. *Healthcare Operations Management.* Chicago: Health Administration Press.

Healthcare Operations Management provides an in-depth examination of contemporary business tools that can be used to improve quality and productivity.

Quality Net. 2011. "Surgical Care Improvement Project." [Online information; retrieved 1/3/11.] www.qualitynet.org/dcs/ContentServer?c=MQParents&pagename=Medqic%2FContent%2FParentShellTemplate&cid=1137346750659&parentName=TopicCat

The Surgical Care Improvement Project (SCIP) is a national quality partnership of organizations focused on improving surgical care by significantly reducing surgical complications.

US Department of Health and Human Services. 2011. "HHS Action Plan to Prevent Healthcare-Associated Infections: Incentives and Oversight." [Online information; retrieved 1/3/11.] www.hhs.gov/ash/initiatives/hai/incentives.html

The Centers for Medicare and Medicaid Services (CMS) has a variety of tools to encourage the prevention of healthcare-associated infections (HAIs). These tools include regulatory oversight, financial incentives, transparency and associated incentives, or some combination of these. Within each of these broad categories are a number of initiatives to combat HAIs, and the HHS website describes the various ways these tools and initiatives support efforts to prevent infections.

Wennberg, D., D. Berkson, and B. Rider. 2008. "Addressing Overuse, Underuse and Misuse of Care." *Healthcare Executive* 23 (4): 8.

This article reports on the survey by the Dartmouth Institute for Health Policy and Clinical Practice, which shows that geography plays a significant role in determining the quality, quantity, and cost of healthcare in the United States. The survey provides the factors that affect variations in practice, which include differences in the way physicians and other caregivers make diagnosis and treatment decisions and measures on the supply side, such as the number of physicians and the availability of hospital beds and imaging technology.

CHAPTER 3

Prevention and Wellness

PREVENTION AND PROGRAMS to promote wellness have always been a part of healthcare in the United States and in some cases have been successful (e.g., in the eradication of smallpox). However, these efforts have been fragmented within federal and state government departments and disconnected from the US healthcare delivery system. The ACA provides a number of new policies to focus and coordinate these efforts and make the connection stronger to healthcare providers and to the public.

The broad system of prevention contains three major elements:

1. Clinical prevention—the routine provision of tests and services (e.g., immunizations) to prevent disease or to uncover and treat it in its early stages
2. Individual wellness—the maintenance of a healthy lifestyle including diet, exercise, and the avoidance of risky behaviors
3. Community building—creating communities that encourage healthy living and strong personal relationships and caring

Exhibit 3.1 illustrates how these policies fit into the systems view of health reform.

CLINICAL PREVENTION

Prevention of disease is a laudable goal—prevention helps individuals live longer and more vital lives and saves money in the system by avoiding unneeded clinical services (e.g., hospitalization for the flu). The savings accrued from prevention can be significant and could reduce cost throughout the system (Maciosek et al. 2010).

Exhibit 3.1 Systems View of Prevention, Wellness, and Community

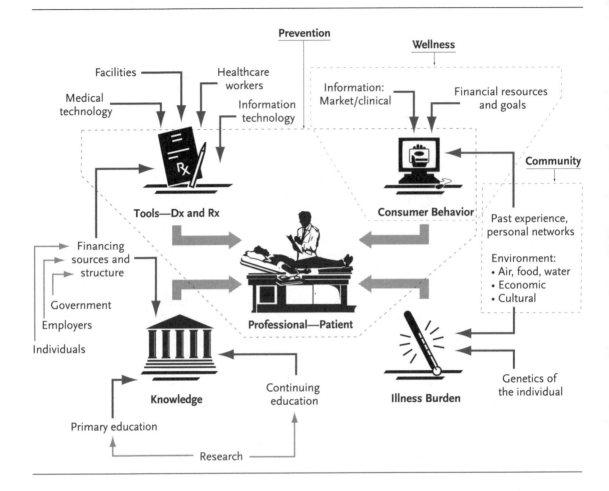

Prevention activities are not yet as widespread as they should be. A recent survey of nearly 1,300 primary care physicians in the United States found that only about 20 percent of them recommend colorectal cancer screening tests to their patients in accordance with current practice guidelines. About 40 percent of the doctors followed some of the practice guidelines, while the remaining 40 percent ignored practice guidelines (Yabroff et al. 2010).

Coordination

Clinical prevention is delivered through a mix of public and private healthcare organizations. Public health departments are responsible for broad prevention activities (e.g., restaurant inspection) and specific programs (e.g., Ryan White Care Act funding for HIV/AIDS prevention).

Most primary care practices adhere to the recommendations of the US Preventive Services Task Force (2011). However, its list of preventive services is long (over 100 services) and some clinicians may not recall an appropriate test or treatment. This challenge is one of the important reasons to install health information technology (HIT) in primary care practices. Almost all HIT systems contain clinical decision support modules that make preventive services recommendations to clinicians at each patient visit.

Title IV of the ACA is solely devoted to prevention and public health. The ACA establishes the National Prevention, Health Promotion, and Public Health Council (§4001) to coordinate federal activities, including substantial new funding. The Preventive Services Task Force continues (§4003) but is augmented with the Community Preventive Services Task Force (§4003), which focuses on population health in addition to the individual needs of each patient.

Title IV also includes a variety of other strategies to improve public health including both school-based clinics (§4101) and oral health (§4102). Title IV adds a Medicare benefit for an annual wellness visit to create a personalized prevention plan (§4103), and removes coinsurance and deductible payments for preventive services. Preventive services for Medicaid recipients are also increased in §4106 and §4107. The elimination of cost sharing for preventive services in private insurance is contained in §4104.

Education

Public education regarding preventive services is enhanced by a federal education and outreach campaign. The focus of the campaign is "nutrition, regular exercise, smoking cessation, obesity reduction, and the five leading killers in the United States" (§4004).

One of the hidden gems of the ACA is the clause in §4003 that states "the campaign . . . may include the use of humor." It is nice to know that the federal government has a sense of humor—at least in this law!

An additional policy to inform the public about health issues is contained in §4205, which requires restaurants with over 20 locations to post the nutritional content of their standard menu items. This section was supported by national restaurant chains because many states and localities were beginning to enact similar requirements, but each with different standards. Under the ACA, one federal standard will be established.

The support for school-based clinics is increased in §4101. In 2009 the Institute of Medicine released a report on "comparative effectiveness research prioritization" (IOM 2009) that listed 100 clinical services that IOM felt should be studied soon because of their variability of application and results. One of these priorities is to "compare the effectiveness of school-based interventions involving meal programs, vending machines, and physical education, at different levels of intensity, in preventing and treating overweight and obesity in children and adolescents." Because of this new emphasis in the ACA, the school may become one of the most effective delivery sites for prevention and wellness education.

WELLNESS

In contrast to clinical prevention, wellness programs are self-directed, and most individuals in the United States are aware of the key elements of wellness:

- An active engagement in routine exercise
- A healthy diet
- Maintenance of a healthy weight
- Avoidance of risky behaviors (smoking, alcohol or drug abuse, driving without seatbelts, etc.)

Unfortunately, residents of the United States have become sedentary and overweight. The ACA promotes wellness though a number of tools.

Employers have been leaders in wellness promotion, with programs to encourage employees to adopt more healthy lifestyles, such as diet counseling, smoking cessation programs, and fitness club memberships. Unfortunately, these voluntary programs have had only limited success (Probart et al. 2010; Schmidt, Voigt, and Wikler 2010). Safeway is a leader with a new approach to wellness that focuses on measurable outcomes such as body mass index, blood pressure, and cholesterol levels. If employees meet specified goals, a substantial portion of their health insurance premium is returned to them as a reward. The effect of this system has been that Safeway had no increase in its health insurance premiums from 2003 to 2008 (no later data have been published) (*The Wall Street Journal* 2009). UnitedHealth Group has implemented a similar system for its 70,000 employees; employees will be eligible for a reward of up to $900 in 2011 (Migliori 2010).

The ACA supports this policy in §2705, which allows employers to reward employees who meet goals a refund of up to 30 percent of the premium cost for the employee. The Secretary of HHS can raise this limit to 50 percent in the future. However, some critics have argued that these systems discriminate against individuals who have preexisting conditions and are physiologically unable to achieve the goals. Therefore this wellness rewards program is a part of §1201/2705 titled "Prohibiting discrimination against individual and beneficiaries based on health status." The remainder of §2705 contains language that prohibits insurance companies from denying coverage to individuals because of preexisting conditions—one of the key goals of health reform.

Medicaid also provides incentives for wellness in §4108. States can establish programs that provide financial rewards to Medicaid beneficiaries for achieving one or more of the following:

- Ceasing use of tobacco products
- Controlling or reducing their weight
- Lowering their cholesterol
- Lowering their blood pressure
- Avoiding the onset of diabetes or, in the case of a person with diabetes, improving the management of that condition

COMMUNITY BUILDING

One of the most accurate predictors of an individual's health status is his or her zip code. Community and public health leaders have long advocated for community building—particularly in those communities challenged by poverty, crime, and poor housing. The ACA accepts this challenge in §4201 with a new program of community transformation grants. The purpose of these grants is to

- create healthier school environments, including increasing healthy food options, physical activity opportunities, promotion of healthy lifestyle, emotional wellness programs, prevention curricula, and activities to prevent chronic diseases;
- create the infrastructure to support active living and access to nutritious foods in a safe environment;
- develop and promote programs targeting a variety of age levels to increase access to nutrition, increase physical activity, encourage smoking cessation, improve social and emotional wellness, and enhance safety in the community;
- assess and implement work-site wellness programming and incentives;
- work to highlight healthy options at restaurants and other food venues;
- prioritize strategies to reduce racial and ethnic disparities, including social, economic, and geographic determinants of health; and

- address special populations needs, including all age groups and individuals with disabilities, and individuals in urban, rural, and frontier areas.

Pilot programs similar to the community transformation grants have been under way for a number of years and are beginning to show significant results. Exhibit 3.2 shows the results of a midpoint review of the California Healthy Eating, Active Communities Program (Samuels et al. 2010). Although these activities may seem far removed from the healthcare delivery system, they actually may be a new market for many providers.

SUMMARY

One of the major causes of the high cost of the US healthcare system is preventable disease and unhealthy lifestyles. The ACA addresses these problems with improved programs of clinical prevention including the requirement that preventive services be offered in all health insurance programs with no cost-sharing requirements. Public education regarding prevention is significantly expanded.

Employer-based wellness programs that reward specific health outcomes have shown success and are carefully supported in the ACA. Requirements are included to ensure that employees are not discriminated against because of preexisting conditions. A similar pilot program is available to Medicaid beneficiaries.

In addition, policies to improve community health are supported through community transformation grants.

Exhibit 3.2 Midpoint Review of the California Healthy Eating, Active Communities (HEAC) Program

Children's Environment	Expected Outcomes	Midpoint Achievements	Midpoint Exposure
School **Goal:** Increase healthy eating and physical activity during the school day	• Adopt and implement state nutrition standards district-wide for a la carte food and beverages sold • Adopt and implement district-wide policies that ensure students receive mandated number of minutes of PE • Engage parents and families as advocates for healthier food and physical activity	• Implemented state nutrition standards (all sites) • Trained classroom teachers on physical activity and hired PE specialists • Adhered to state requirement for PE minutes and expanded class time • Used technical assistance and resources from public health departments and healthcare sector to accomplish goals • Parents involved in changing food and physical activity environments through participation in wellness policy committees	• 11 school districts • 885,000 elementary, middle, and high school students • 769,000 students exposed to intensive PE interventions
After School **Goal:** Increase healthy eating and physical activity in after-school programs	• Adopt and implement SB 12, SB 965, or other policies[1] that make healthy foods accessible in after-school sites • Adopt and implement policies that promote physical activity on a regular basis • Engage parents and youth as advocates for healthier food and physical activity in after-school settings	• Secured state after-school funding • Hired after-school coordinator • Included physical activity in "higher learning" (academic) after-school sites • Introduced SPARK physical activity curriculum in after-school programs	• 14 after-school programs • 7,000 enrolled participants • 3,900 after-school sites statewide required to adopt HEAC strategies, adhere to state nutrition standards, and document nutrition and physical activity environments

(Continued)

Prevention and Wellness   43

Exhibit 3.2 *(Continued)*

Children's Environment	Expected Outcomes	Midpoint Achievements	Midpoint Exposure
Neighborhood **Goal:** Increase children's and families' opportunities for healthy eating and physical activity in neighborhoods	• Policies and programs lead to improved access to affordable, quality, healthy food • Policies and programs lead to improved access to physical activity opportunities • Residents develop increased policy advocacy capacity	• Created "healthy check-out lines" (WalMart, Smart & Final) • Convinced convenience stores to sell produce and healthier foods • Improved parks and advocated for updated park equipment and programming • Improved walkability and bikeability around schools; created complete streets policies	• 470,000 residents in 6 HEAC communities have been exposed to HEAC food retail interventions
Healthcare **Goal:** Engage local healthcare systems in diabetes and obesity prevention	• Healthcare spokespersons are testifying at school board meetings, planning commission meetings, and city council meetings • Promotoras[2] have a prominent role as health liaisons with the community • Healthcare providers incorporate obesity prevention into well-child visits • Healthcare agencies have organizational policies that promote healthy eating and physical activity	• Trained, educated, and recruited physicians and promotoras for obesity prevention and policy advocacy • Implemented weight management programs such as KP Kids and Kidshape • Developed county vending policies and healthy hospital policies (all sites) • Changed clinical practices to include BMI charting and obesity prevention messages • Implemented policy for drug representatives to provide healthy foods to healthcare practices	• More than 300 healthcare providers have been exposed to HEAC clinical training and community programs on childhood obesity prevention

Exhibit 3.2 *(Continued)*

Children's Environment	Expected Outcomes	Midpoint Achievements	Midpoint Exposure
Marketing and Advertising **Goal:** Discourage or eliminate local-level advertising and marketing of unhealthy foods and beverages and inactivity in school, after-school, and neighborhood settings, and encourage regulatory action to reduce advertising to children	• Reduce or eliminate neighborhood-level marketing to children • Local marketing is assessed, and youth are active in advocating for reducing marketing of unhealthy foods • Tell parents how some businesses market unhealthy food and physical activity to children	• Included ban on unhealthy food marketing within district wellness policies • Engaged youth in assessing marketing environments in schools and local stores • Worked to get healthy advertising into new stadium • Implemented soda-free summer campaign	• 276 students have been engaged in HEAC youth leadership programs, conducting assessments and reporting on food and physical activity environments

1. In 2005, California passed laws setting minimum nutritional standards for a la carte food and beverages sold on school campuses. Law SB 12 sets standards for all competitive foods sold on public school campuses for grades K–12. For food items, fat content is not to exceed 35% of calories, saturated fat content is not to exceed 10% of calories, and sugar content is not to exceed 35% of total weight of food. SB 965 sets standards for beverages sold on public school campuses for grades K–12. Beverages allowed for sale at middle and high schools are fruit drinks made of 50% or more fruit juice with no added sweetener, water, milk products, and certain electrolyte replacement beverages.

2. Promotoras are outreach workers in Hispanic communities who are responsible for raising awareness of health and educational issues.

Source: Used with permission from the American Public Health Association. Samuels, S. E., L. Craypo, M. Boyle, P. B. Crawford, A. Yancy, and G. Flores. 2010. "The California Endowment's Healthy Eating, Active Communities Program: A Midpoint Review." *American Journal of Public Health* 100 (11): 2114–23.

ANNOTATED REFERENCES

Institute of Medicine (IOM). 2009. "Initial National Priorities for Comparative Effectiveness Research Report Brief." [Online brief; published June 2009.] www.iom.edu/~/media/ Files/Report%20Files/2009/ComparativeEffectivenessResearchPriorities/CER%20report% 20brief%2008-13-09.ashx

In the American Recovery and Reinvestment Act, the Institute of Medicine (IOM) was asked to recommend national priorities for research questions to be addressed by comparative effectiveness research (CER) and supported by ARRA funds. The IOM committee identified three report objectives: (1) establish a working definition of CER, (2) develop a priority list of research topics to be undertaken with ARRA funding using broad stakeholder input, and (3) identify the necessary requirements to support a robust and sustainable CER enterprise. The results of the work provide the initial list in the report brief.

Maciosek, M. V., A. B. Coffield, T. J. Flottemesch, N. M. Edwards, and L. I. Solberg. 2010. "Greater Use of Preventive Services in U.S. Health Care Could Save Lives at Little or No Cost." *Health Affairs* 29 (9): 1656.

Abstract: There is broad debate over whether preventive health services save money or represent a good investment. This article analyzes the estimated cost of adopting a package of 20 proven preventive services—including tobacco cessation screening, alcohol abuse screening, and daily aspirin use—against the estimated savings that could be generated. We find that greater use of proven clinical preventive services in the United States could avert the loss of more than two million life years annually. What's more, increasing the use of these services from current levels to 90 percent in 2006 would result in total savings of $3.7 billion, or 0.2 percent of US personal healthcare spending. These findings suggest that policymakers should pursue options that move the nation toward greater use of proven preventive services.

Migliori, R. 2010. Keynote speaker at Midwest Healthcare Business Intelligence Summit, October 19.

Probart, C., E. T. McDonnell, L. Jomaa, and V. Fekete. 2010. "Lessons from Pennsylvania's Mixed Response to Federal School Wellness Law." *Health Affairs* 29 (3): 447.

Abstract: Federal legislation aimed at tackling the nation's soaring childhood obesity rate through changes to school meals and nutrition and wellness programs has met with mixed results. An examination of Pennsylvania's response to the Child Nutrition and Women, Infants, and Children (WIC) Reauthorization Act of 2004, one of the most comprehensive state responses, found improvements to the nutritional quality of foods offered à la carte in conjunction with school meal programs. However, multiple weaknesses remain. Consistent wellness policy implementation steps were not followed, and there was inadequate statewide enforcement. Despite this, Pennsylvania can offer lessons for other states in moving forward with programs to promote good nutrition and wellness.

Samuels, S. E., L. Craypo, M. Boyle, P. B. Crawford, A. Yancy, and G. Flores. 2010. "The California Endowment's Healthy Eating, Active Communities Program: A Midpoint Review." *American Journal of Public Health* 100 (11): 2114–23.

Schmidt, H., K. Voigt, and D. Wikler. 2010. "Carrots, Sticks, and Health Care Reform— Problems with Wellness Incentives." *New England Journal of Medicine* 362 (2).

Excerpt: Chronic conditions, especially those associated with overweight, are on the rise in the United States (as elsewhere). Employers have used carrots and sticks to encourage healthier behavior. The current healthcare reform bills seek to expand the role of incentives, which promise a win–win bargain: employees enjoy better health, while employers reduce healthcare costs and profit from a healthier workforce. However, these provisions cannot be given an ethical free pass. In some cases, the incentives are really sticks dressed up as carrots. There is a risk of inequity that would further disadvantage the people most in need of health improvements, and doctors might be assigned watchdog roles that might harm the therapeutic relationship. We believe that some changes must be made to reconcile incentive use with ethical norms.

US Preventive Services Task Force. 2011. "Recommendations." [Online information; retrieved 1/7/11.] www.uspreventiveservicestaskforce.org/recommendations.htm

The US Preventive Services Task Force (USPSTF) is an independent panel of non-federal experts in prevention and evidence-based medicine and is composed of primary care providers (such as internists, pediatricians, family physicians, gynecologists/obstetricians, nurses, and health behavior specialists). The USPSTF conducts scientific evidence reviews of a broad range of clinical preventive healthcare services (such as screening, counseling, and preventive medications) and develops recommendations for primary care clinicians and health systems. These recommendations are published in the form of "Recommendation Statements."

The Wall Street Journal. 2009. "How Safeway Is Cutting Health-Care Costs." [Online article; published 6/12/09.] http://online.wsj.com/article/SB124476804026308603.html

Steven A. Burd, CEO of Safeway, wrote an article for The Wall Street Journal about its wellness program.

"At Safeway we believe that well-designed healthcare reform, utilizing market-based solutions, can ultimately reduce our nation's healthcare bill by 40%. The key to achieving these savings is healthcare plans that reward healthy behavior. As a self-insured employer, Safeway designed just such a plan in 2005 and has made continuous improvements each year. The results have been remarkable. During this four-year period, we have kept our per capita healthcare costs flat (that includes the employee and the employer portion), while most American companies' costs have increased 38% over the same four years."

Yabroff, K. R., C. N. Klabunde, G. Yuan, T. S. McNeel, M. L. Brown, D. Casciotti, D. W. Buckman, and S. Taplan. 2010. "Are Physicians' Recommendations for Colorectal Cancer Screening Guideline-Consistent?" Journal of General Internal Medicine 26 (2): 177–84.

In 2010 a study found that about 40 percent of the doctors followed some of the practice guidelines, while 40 percent ignored practice guidelines. The National Cancer Institute and HealthLeaders Media published press releases covering the study: http://www.cancer.gov/newscenter/pressreleases/ColorectalCancerScreeningPhysicians and http://www.healthleadersmedia.com/content/PHY-257796/Most-Physicians-Fail-to-Follow-CRC-Screening-Guidelines##

CHAPTER 4

Systems View Scenarios

IN THE INTRODUCTION, scenario planning was presented as an aid to strategy formulation. In scenario planning, two significant policies or market trends with uncertain effects on healthcare are identified. These two trends are then arrayed in a scenario cross to create four unique scenarios that are named and described in short paragraphs. Finally, strategy options are created and tested against each scenario to determine which options are likely to succeed in the highest number of scenarios. Scenario planning is used in this chapter to create scenarios around chronic disease management and consumer engagement in wellness and prevention.

CHRONIC DISEASE MANAGEMENT

Health Information Technology and Primary Care Providers

An important policy goal of the ACA is to improve chronic disease management. Two major policies are included in the ACA and the American Recovery and Reinvestment Act of 2009 (ARRA) to meet this goal—the increased use of health information technology (HIT) and an increased supply of primary care physicians.

The ARRA provided significant funding for the installation of HIT in hospitals and doctor's clinics. The ACA integrates HIT use in many sections of the law. Unfortunately, HIT literature contains a number of examples of the ineffective installation and use of these systems (DesRoches et al. 2010; Frisse 2009), so their usefulness for chronic disease management is certainly not assured. For example, the installation of HIT does not always solve broken medical records processes, eliminate chart reconciliation or lost data, or totally eliminate paper systems.

The second important policy in the ACA to improve chronic disease management is to increase the supply of primary care physicians. Although most policy analysts agree that an increased primary care workforce is necessary for reform to succeed, lower salaries for primary care physicians may still depress their supply. A recent salary survey shows a remarkable gap between primary care and specialty physician salaries (StudentDoc 2011). For example, the average salary for family physicians reported in January 2011 was $204,000, in contrast to the average salary for cardiologists, which was $403,000.

The scenario cross for these two policies is displayed in Exhibit 4.1.

Scenarios

1. Robots for All

The installation and use of HIT has gone smoothly and many organizations have developed sophisticated data warehouses and analytical tools. The supply of primary care physicians has declined and primary care services are increasingly delivered by nurses and other practitioners. The medical home concept is widely used and its definition has been expanded. Many patients with chronic disease use online computer-based algorithms to monitor their care, adjust their medications, and help them determine when they need to see a specialist.

2. The Cost Curve Bends

Three major features are integrated into the care of patients with chronic disease. HIT systems employ sophisticated applications that alert providers when care needs to be modified. The supply of primary care physicians and advanced practice nurses is adequate so patient loads are manageable and new patients can find primary care services easily. The medical home model is effectively deployed and providers' income and satisfaction have increased. The amount of healthcare resources—including drugs, devices, and imaging—being consumed has decreased. Of particular interest is a 30 percent decline in hospital patient days.

3. Status Quo

HIT implementation remains slow and in some areas does not occur, as providers have decided that the cost of implementation is not justified because of payment changes in Medicare. The primary care workforce remains small and continues to decline. Consumers choose retail healthcare

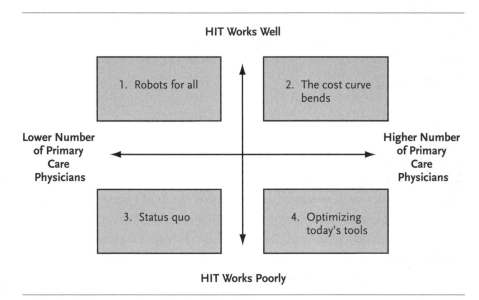

Exhibit 4.1
Scenario Cross
for Chronic
Disease
Management

HIT Works Well

1. Robots for all	2. The cost curve bends

Lower Number of Primary Care Physicians ←——————————→ Higher Number of Primary Care Physicians

3. Status quo	4. Optimizing today's tools

HIT Works Poorly

for minor problems and go directly to specialists for more serious issues. Many consumers engage in "do it yourself" healthcare through the use of Web resources such as patientslikeme.com (2011).

4. Optimizing Today's Tools

HIT implementation remains slow and in some areas does not occur, as providers have decided the cost of implementation is not justified because of payment changes. Newly developed paper systems provide registries for chronic patients; many of these newer manual systems were developed through sophisticated Lean Six Sigma projects and are distributed by national retail chains such as WalMart and Target. The supply of primary care physicians and advanced practice nurses is adequate. Because the paper systems save money by avoiding automation, clerical staff and transcribers have been added.

Strategy Options

The challenge of chronic disease management can be met with a number of organizational strategies. Most will be led by hospitals, but entrepreneurial doctors are also likely to develop new structures to meet this challenge and opportunity.

1. Hospital and Doctors Form a Fully Integrated System

A clear option for hospitals and doctors (and in some cases health plans) is to become a fully integrated system (e.g., Mayo Clinic, Cleveland Clinic).

This structure is well suited to scenarios 1 and 2 but does not have significant competitive advantage for scenarios 3 and 4. Forming large systems is difficult, which is reflected by the small number of these organizations operating today.

2. Hospitals Develop ACOs and Then Become Risk Bearing

Another less intense integration option is for a hospital and its physicians to form an accountable care organization (see Chapter 5). In this model, the ACO provides care to a defined set of Medicare patients, and if their aggregate cost is less than a target set by Medicare, the ACO keeps a portion of the savings (§3022). The ACO model also works well with scenarios 1 and 2 but not as effectively in scenario 2 as a fully integrated system does. Controlling some patient care services is difficult when physicians are not employed by the ACO. The model can succeed in scenarios 3 and 4 but may lose money in scenario 3 if the ACO does not succeed in meeting its cost targets.

3. Hospitals Hire Primary Care Physicians—Specialists Remain Independent

Increasingly, hospitals employ primary care physicians (Crosson and Tollen 2010). This strategy is conservative and somewhat defensive but also has low risk. However, employment is not necessarily a successful strategy for scenarios 1 and 2, as the exclusion of specialty physicians makes the effective use of HIT difficult. Employment of primary care physicians is successful for scenarios 3 and 4 and may be an excellent interim strategic stance for one to three years.

4. Physicians Develop Alternative Care Models Independent of Hospitals

Physicians will not be passive as the ACA takes effect, and many will resist working for the hospital. Therefore, physicians will develop new systems of care beyond traditional office visits such as retail clinics, e-visits, concierge care, private-pay only, and stand-alone emergency centers. These strategies may be effective for scenarios 1 and 3 with the decreased availability of primary care. They might also work well for scenario 4, as many of today's management and clinical tools are not fully utilized, and smaller, nimble practices can make effective change quickly. However, this strategy will probably not be successful in scenario 2, as truly effective chronic disease management requires some integration and coordination for all parts of the system.

Additional strategy options can be found at the companion website at ache.org/books/reform.

CONSUMER ENGAGEMENT

Prevention and Wellness

One of the important goals of the ACA from a systems perspective is to engage consumers at a new level in the maintenance and improvement of their own health. During the legislative process, the administration vacillated between calling the ACA "health reform" and "health insurance reform." The final product truly is health reform, as it has many policies that go beyond the effective functioning of the health insurance system (see Chapter 3).

Two aspects of consumer engagement have high levels of uncertain effectiveness:

1. How well consumers personally engage in the prevention strategies in the ACA
2. How well employees respond to wellness incentives offered by their employers

Prevention, which seeks to prevent or discover specific diseases, must be distinguished from wellness, which is focused on keeping the body generally fit and in prime condition (Exhibit 4.2).

Scenarios

1. Healthy but Out of Shape
Prevention programs have increased in effectiveness—particularly because the ACA has mandated that preventive services are covered fully. Even though employers provide significant financial incentives for employees to develop healthy lifestyles, obesity continues as the major health concern in the United States.

2. Hale and Hearty
Wellness and prevention programs work well and the primary causes of disease are genetically based. Many individuals maintain a high level of health and vitality into their nineties. Hospital days and visits to physicians decrease by 30 percent.

3. Overweight and Sick
Although preventive services are fully covered, many individuals do not use these services because of lack of awareness and the inconvenience of

Exhibit 4.2
Scenario Cross
for Prevention
and Wellness

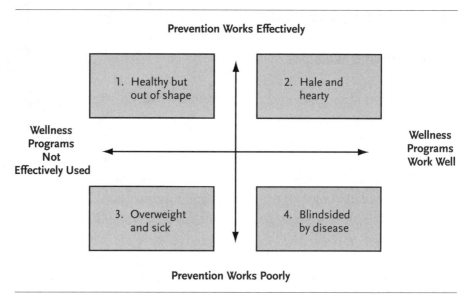

some of the tests (e.g., colonoscopy). Employer-based wellness programs are ineffective. The incidence of chronic disease rises, as does the demand for inpatient and physician services.

4. Blindsided by Disease

Preventive services are not effectively used by most consumers, who believe that staying in shape is all that is needed for a healthy life. In most cases individuals keep their weight under control, maintain an excellent blood pressure and cholesterol level, and don't smoke or abuse any substances. The incidence of some chronic diseases such as diabetes decreases but the incidence of late-stage cancer and infectious disease rises.

Strategies

Although most healthcare delivery organizations have not put significant emphasis on prevention and wellness programs, a number of new strategic possibilities now arise.

1. Providers Make Connections to Retail Clinics

Healthcare is clearly moving to more retail environments (e.g., WalMart, Target, CVS), and patients have less loyalty to individual physicians (Wilson et al. 2010). A health system (hospitals and doctors affiliated in some manner) could be the provider of services to the retail site. In some cases, a more comprehensive clinic might be installed to provide greater value to the customer. This strategy would work well for scenarios 1 and 2 if preventive services were offered on-site (e.g., flu shots). A more comprehensive clinic would be needed for scenarios 3 and 4 as more of the work of the clinic would be diagnostic (and in some instances would include a referral to a hospital emergency department).

2. Providers Make Connections to Public Health Agencies

Historically, public health programs have been operated by state or local government and have been categorically focused (e.g, HIV/AIDS or maternal and child care); however, with the broader definition of health contained in the ACA, general interest in wellness and prevention will increase. Therefore, a health system could partner with local public health agencies to offer services that wrap around traditional public health programs. For example, maternal and child services (HHS 2011) could be provided for the general population in addition to those children who are categorically eligible. This strategy could work well for scenarios 3 and 4, where additional prevention outreach will be needed.

3. Providers Develop or Partner with Work-Site Wellness Programs

As employers provide more incentives for employees to maintain healthy lifestyles, healthcare systems may wish to enter the work-site wellness market (Smerd 2010). Although these services may not be highly profitable, they will provide branding for the organization and a simplified referral system for higher-level services. This strategy would work well for scenarios 2 and 4.

4. Providers Develop and Staff Employer-Based Clinics

The work-site wellness program can be complemented by on-site clinics (yes—back to the company doctor!). This work-site clinic could be modeled on the retail clinics described in the first strategy. This strategy could work well for all four scenarios.

More strategies related to consumer engagement can be found at the companion website (ache.org/books/reform).

SUMMARY

The chronic disease management scenario contains two major uncertainties: the use of HIT and the supply of primary care providers. Potential strategies for this future include

1. hospitals and doctors form fully integrated systems,
2. hospitals develop ACOs and become risk bearing,

3. hospitals hire primary physicians, but specialists remain independent, and

4. physicians develop alternative care models independent of hospitals.

The consumer engagement scenario contains two major uncertainties: prevention and wellness. Potential strategies for this future include

1. providers make connections to retail clinics,
2. providers make connections to public health agencies,
3. providers develop or partner with work-site wellness programs, and
4. providers develop and staff employer-based clinics.

ANNOTATED REFERENCES

Crosson, F. J., and L. A. Tollen. 2010. *Partners in Health: How Physicians and Hospitals Can Be Accountable Together*, 31. San Francisco: Jossey-Bass.

DesRoches, C. M., E. G. Campbell, C. Vogeli, J. Zheng, S. R. Rao, A. E. Shields, K. Donelan, S. Rosenbaum, S. J. Bristol, and A. K. Jha. 2010. "Electronic Health Records' Limited Successes Suggest More Targeted Uses." *Health Affairs* 29 (4): 639.

Frisse, M. E. 2009. "Health Information Technology: One Step at a Time." *Health Affairs* 28 (2): w379.

Patientslikeme.com. 2011. [Online information; retrieved 1/7/11.] www.patientslikeme.com/
   Patients Like Me is focused on individuals with life-changing conditions. Its intent is for patients to learn from the real-world experiences of other similar patients.

Smerd, J. 2010. "Work-Site Clinics Gaining Favor as Retail Locations Lag." *Workforce Management* 89 (4): 8.

StudentDoc. 2011. "Physician Salaries—Salary Survey Results." [Online information; retrieved 1/7/11.] www.studentdoc.com/salaries.html
   The StudentDoc website maintains an active survey of current salaries paid for each specialty.

US Department of Health and Human Services (HHS). 2011. "Maternal and Child Health Bureau." [Online information; retrieved 1/7/11.] http://mchb.hrsa.gov/
   The federal Health Resources and Services Administration funds and oversees this program.

Wilson, A. R., X. T. Zhou, W. Shi, H. Rodin, E. P. Bargman, N. A. Garrett, and T. J. Sandberg. 2010. "Retail Clinic Versus Office Setting: Do Patients Choose Appropriate Providers?" *American Journal of Managed Care* 16 (10): 753.

PART 2

Funds Flow and Incentives

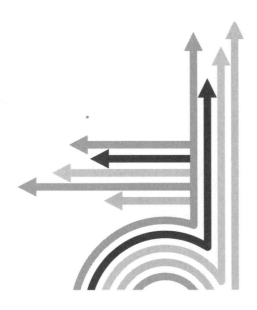

CHAPTER 5

Payment Incentives

THE SECOND MAJOR theory that underlies the ACA is the use of payment incentives to drive behavior. Payment policies in the ACA are projected to save significant Medicare expenditures from otherwise expected cost increases. This "bending of the cost curve" is demonstrated in Exhibit 5.1. The payment policies that accomplish these savings can be broadly grouped into four areas:

1. Reduced total cost of care through improved chronic care management
2. Reduced inpatient use and cost per admission
3. Reduced fraud and abuse
4. Reduced payment to providers (see Chapter 2)

Medicare policy drives almost all other payer policy and therefore the Medicare (and Medicaid) payment incentives contained in the ACA will improve all healthcare delivery in the United States.

Although private payers will experiment with different payment systems, most providers design their operations to maximize payment from Medicare and Medicare. Designing and improving patient care systems that provide quality care and maximize payment for one payment system is difficult; trying to create different patient care processes for multiple payers is nearly impossible. The one salient exception is formularies where different payers cover different drugs. However, these differences may diminish in the future.

Many areas of the United States deliver higher-quality and lower-cost care than others because of their more efficient use of healthcare services. The ACA was crafted with the belief that the whole system can be made more effective and efficient by encouraging the spread of these more efficient

Exhibit 5.1
Medicare
Spending with
and Without
Reform

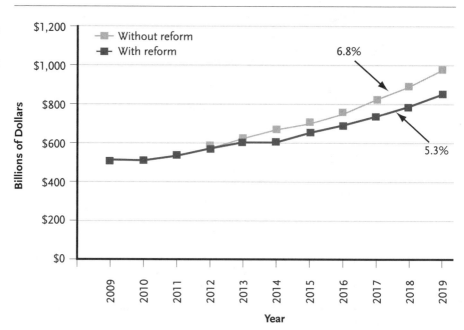

Source: Analysis based on data from the CMS Office of the Actuary's April 22, 2010, report. "Estimated Financial Effects of the "Patient Protection and Affordable Care Act," as amended. www.cms.gov/ActuarialStudies/05_HealthCareReform.asp

practices throughout the nation. However, some policymakers have raised concerns that policies that provide incentives for efficiency can lead to rationing. The experiences with tightly managed HMOs in the 1980s and 1990s provided some highly public examples of patients being denied care because of the financial incentives inherent in health plan management (Blendon et al. 1998; Bodenheimer and Pham 2010).

The antidote to this problem is quality reporting. Quality measurement and public reporting have matured significantly in the past 20 years. The federal website Healthcare.gov provides patients and providers with numerous metrics to evaluate performance in three spheres: clinical quality, safety, and patient experience. In addition, state-based quality-reporting organizations are becoming more widespread and useful to consumers (see Wisconsin Collaborative for Healthcare Quality 2011; MN Community Measurement 2011; and Health Care Cost and Quality Council at Mass.gov 2011). Quality-reporting systems have matured to the point that the authors of the ACA felt comfortable including payment incentives in the final law.

Payment policies can be characterized as incentives (carrots) and penalties (sticks). Unfortunately, fraud continues to plague the Medicare system and therefore a number of new policies in the ACA incent providers to fully comply with Medicare payment rules.

In addition to specific payment policies that will be implemented between 2011 and 2014, the ACA contains more general features to improve payment in the future (i.e., Center for Medicare and Medicaid Innovation) or take a stronger hand to control costs (i.e., Independent Payment Advisory Board). These payment polices are explored in the following sections.

INCENTIVES—THE CARROTS

Accountable Care Organizations

One of the more highly publicized portions of the ACA is the newly created shared savings program for Medicare: the accountable care organization (§3022). (The ACA also includes an ACO for Pediatric Medicaid patients in §2706.) The ACO concept was based on proposals from Fisher and colleagues (2009) at Dartmouth and by the results of the Medicare Group Practice Demonstration Project (MedPAC 2009).

The basic principle of an ACO is that a group of providers becomes accountable for the care—including quality and cost—of a specific population. If the quality goals are met and the cost is less than the target set by the payer, the savings are shared, hence the name "shared savings." Three advantages for providers are inherent in the ACA version of ACOs. First, the capitation risk is removed as providers receive their normal fee-for-service payments plus a bonus if cost and quality targets are met. Second, patients need not enroll, as Medicare automatically includes them as part of a specific ACO based on their choice of providers. Third, ACOs need not be fully integrated healthcare systems, as more loosely structured organizations can be used (e.g., physician hospital organizations [PHOs]). Thorpe and Ogden (2010) have called these looser structures "virtual integrated systems." The final form of the ACOs will depend on regulations written by HHS before the start date, which is no later than 2012. Medicare ACOs have specific requirements (Fisher et al. 2009):

- ACOs must have a formal legal structure to receive and distribute shared savings to participating providers.
- Each ACO must employ enough primary care professionals to treat its beneficiary population (minimum of 5,000 beneficiaries). CMS decides how many is sufficient.
- Each ACO must agree to at least three years of participation in the program.

- Each ACO will develop sufficient information about its participating healthcare professionals to support beneficiary assignment and for the determination of payments for shared savings.
- ACOs will be expected to include a leadership and management structure that includes clinical and administrative systems.
- Each ACO will be expected to have defined processes to promote evidence-based medicine, report on quality and cost measures, and coordinate care.
- ACOs will be required to produce reports demonstrating the adoption of patient-centered care.

An interesting addition to §3022 is the ability of HHS to provide partial capitation to selected ACOs. Partial capitation could be for ambulatory care only or other selected services. This provides an interesting entry for ACOs into areas previously reserved for health plans.

Implementing ACOs includes some challenges:

- ACOs will only succeed with chronic disease management (see Chapter 1) that minimizes preventable conditions, acute care episodes, and complicated inpatient admissions.
- Legal structures need to be developed to allow full participation and cooperation by all providers in an ACO.
- The shared savings model does not provide up-front funding, so initial capital must be found to fund the systems (people and HIT) needed to perform well in chronic disease management.
- The leadership of newly formed ACOs must be exceptionally skilled to bring together providers who have not had a history of effectively working together.

The Marshfield Clinic was one of the most successful participants in the Physician Group Practice (PGP) Demonstration, which was sponsored by CMS and was the precursor to the structures and financing of ACOs in the ACA. By year three of the PGP Demonstration Marshfield had met greater than 98 percent of the 32 quality measures (measures regarding diabetes, heart failure, coronary artery disease, hypertension, and preventive services) and received a performance payment of $13.8 million. Savings to Medicare in that year were $23.49 million (Praxel 2009).

Marshfield Clinic staff attribute much of their success to their mature HIT and electronic health record. The *New York Times* reported in 2008:

> The Medicare pilot prompted Marshfield to take a fresh look at how it cares for various chronic conditions, including heart disease and hypertension.

That led to a new software tool, called the iList, which has proved a big help, said Dr. Theodore A. Praxel, Marshfield's medical director of quality improvement and care management. The iList (for "intervention list") culls the patient records of a primary care physician and ranks and flags patients by conditions not met, including uncontrolled blood pressure and cholesterol, overdue lab tests and vaccinations. Nurses and medical assistants then "work the iList," calling patients with reminders and scheduling them for exams and lab work.

In medicine, the computer is to memory what the X-ray machine is to vision—a technology that vastly surpasses human limitations. The benefits of a computer-helper, doctors say, become quickly evident in everyday practice. (Lohr 2008)

The Congressional Budget Office has projected that ACOs will reduce Medicare spending by nearly $5 billion over the next ten years. CMS is working to make the program operational by January 1, 2012 (CMS/Office of Legislation 2011).

Bundled Payments

Bundled payments are another mechanism for making providers accountable for care. Bundled payments are included in the ACA in §3023. In this payment pilot an organization takes on the responsibility for costs and quality for an episode of inpatient care.

The bundled payment policy is based on the positive results of the Medicare Acute Care Episode (ACE) Demonstration (CMS 2011). The ACE program pays a flat bundled rate for 9 orthopedic and 28 cardiac procedures. This fee includes hospital care, physician fees, and outpatient follow-up and rehabilitation. Twenty-two quality measures are reported each quarter to CMS. Physician payments can be increased by 25 percent if certain cost reduction targets and quality goals are met. Interestingly, patients are also paid a bonus of up to $1,157 to participate in the ACE project, but this payment is not part of ACA §3023 and §2704. The Baptist Health system in Texas participated in the ACE project and received gain-sharing payments from Medicare that ranged from $65 to $6,000 per admission (My San Antonio 2009).

The ACA significantly expands the number of conditions that will be part of the bundled payment project. These conditions will include a mix of chronic and acute conditions—surgical and medical—and will be conditions for which an opportunity for quality improvement and reduced expenditures exists. The conditions chosen will vary in the number of readmissions, the amount of expenditures for post–acute care spending, and whether the condition is amenable to bundling across the spectrum of care.

Organizations that can participate are composed of providers of services and suppliers, including hospitals, physician groups, skilled nursing facilities (SNFs), and home health agencies. Because these organizations can be structured in numerous ways, they face the same organizational and funding challenges of ACOs. The bundling pilot starts in 2013.

PENALTIES—THE STICK

The ACA also contains sections intended to reduce unwanted behaviors or results.

In 2007 MedPAC reported that 17.6 percent of hospital admissions resulted in readmissions within 30 days of discharge, 11.3 percent within 15 days, and 6.2 percent within 7 days. MedPAC found that Medicare spends about $12 billion annually on potentially preventable readmissions. In addition, variation in readmission rates by hospital and geographic region suggests that some hospitals and geographic areas are better than others at containing readmission rates (MedPAC 2007).

Therefore, §3025 contains a new and complex payment adjustment to provide incentives for hospitals to reduce the rate of unnecessary readmission. Hospitals with "excessive" 30-day readmissions for specified conditions will incur financial penalties starting fiscal years (FY) beginning after October 1, 2012. Three high-volume/high-cost conditions (heart attack, heart failure, and pneumonia) will be designated by HHS, and four more conditions, such as chronic obstructive pulmonary disorder and cardiac and vascular surgical procedures, may be added in 2015.

The base inpatient payment for hospitals with readmission rates higher than Medicare-calculated expected readmission rates will be reduced by an adjustment factor that is the greater of

- a hospital-specific readjustment factor based on the number of readmitted patients in excess of the hospital's calculated expected readmission rate, or
- 0.99 in FY 2013; 0.98 in FY 2014; and 0.97 in FY 2015 and beyond.

MedPAC suggests a number of ways hospitals can reduce readmissions based on best practices of leading hospitals (MedPAC 2007, 111):

- Provide better, safer care during the inpatient stay

- Attend to the patient's medication needs at discharge
- Improve communication with patients before and after discharge
- Improve communications with other providers
- Review and improve practice patterns

Hospital-Acquired Conditions

Unfortunately, approximately 1 in 20 patients admitted to a hospital for routine surgery or other treatment pick up serious infections that they did not have at the time of admission. These infections can lengthen stays and may cause death. In a survey of the problem, policy analyst Ramanan Laxminarayan (2010) found that

> In 2006 alone, some 290,000 people contracted bloodstream infections (sepsis) and another 200,000 caught pneumonia while in US hospitals. Their hospital stays were extended by 2.3 million patient-days. The cost: $8.1 billion and 48,000 deaths, all preventable.
>
> One reason for the high mortality rate is that common infections have become resistant to some antibiotics. *Staphylococcus aureus,* especially methicillin-resistant *S. aureus* (MRSA), is the primary cause of lower respiratory tract infections and surgical site infections. MRSA is now endemic, and even epidemic, in many US hospitals, but it is not the only problematic pathogen. Increasingly, resistant strains of enterococci and gram-negative bacteria such as *Pseudomonas aeruginosa* and *Klebsiella pneumoniae* are infecting hospital patients. Resistant pathogens persist in hospitals because of excessive antibiotic use, high susceptibility of patients, and colonization of hospital staff or the hospital environment. They are then carried to other facilities by colonized patients.
>
> The root cause of the problem is the lack of infection control, which in turn is caused by the lack of incentives to do something about it. Hospitals don't pay the full costs of treating cases of infection because they can charge third-party payers for infections regardless of their origin. (Laxminarayan 2010; printed with permission from rrf.org)

The ACA addresses this problem in §3008 by reducing Medicare payment to some hospitals. Hospitals are first ranked on the number of hospital-acquired conditions per discharge. For hospitals in the top quartile of this ranking, their Medicare payment rate is reduced by 1 percent. The ACA also prohibits Medicaid payments completely for healthcare-acquired conditions (HACs) in §2702. After 2012, these policies may be expanded to many other facilities under the Medicare program, including inpatient rehabilitation facilities, long-term-care hospitals, SNFs, ambulatory surgical centers (ASCs), and health clinics.

FRAUD AND ABUSE—THE BIG STICK

Medicare and Medicaid fraud is rampant in some areas of the country (Allen 2007).

In 2007 National Public Radio reported "fraudulent Medicare claims estimated at between $300 million and $400 million were prosecuted in two South Florida counties in the past year. And those are just the cases that have drawn the attention of the courts. Estimates of total losses range as high as 10 times that much" (Allen 2007).

Many new policies are included in Title V of the ACA to combat this problem. They are too numerous to list in this book but a few will cause notable disruptions in some administrative and care processes. New provider screening rules are enacted in §6401 to prevent fraudulent providers from receiving payments; §6402 authorizes the use of advanced data mining techniques to uncover patterns of billing that may be fraudulent; §6406 requires that physician and other suppliers maintain documentation relating to written orders or requests for payment for durable medical equipment, certifications for home health services, or referrals to suppliers.

Section §6407 mandates a face-to-face encounter with a patient before physicians can certify eligibility for home health services or durable medical equipment, changing a simple phone call into a clinic visit that will clearly reduce fraud but may also reduce the use of needed services.

Recovery Audit Contractors (RAC)

In 2008 CMS reported that it had identified nearly $1.03 billion in improper Medicare payments since the Recovery Audit Contractors (RAC) program began in 2005. Approximately 96 percent of the improper payments ($992.7 million) identified by the RACs were overpayments collected from healthcare providers; the remaining 4 percent ($37.8 million) were underpayments repaid to healthcare providers. Most overpayments occur when providers do not comply with Medicare's coding or medical necessity policies (CMS 2008). This program is expanded to Medicaid in §6411.

The most successful solution to fraud is not contained in this title of the ACA, but rather in portions of the ACA that reward "systems-based care."

When providers are organized to provide coordinated care and have transparent systems to monitor funds flow in their systems, the opportunities for fraud are significantly diminished.

THE BACKUP PLANS

Because the ACA was enacted in a very intense environment, not every payment policy strategy could be included. Therefore, two new organizations were included to improve the ACA in the future.

Center for Medicare and Medicaid Innovation

Although CMS has initiated a number of pilots and demonstration projects in the past, it has encountered two problems. First, the programs must be budget neutral, which is challenging in that some concepts take many years before they can achieve this goal. Second, for demonstrations to become a permanent part of CMS policy, they need to be enacted by Congress. These obstacles are removed with the creation of the Center for Medicare and Medicaid Innovation (CMI, §3021), where budget neutrality is not required and the CMI can move successful pilots directly into permanent CMS policy.

The purpose of the CMI is to test innovative payment and service delivery models to reduce Medicare and Medicaid expenditures while preserving or enhancing the quality of care. The CMI will give preference to models that also improve the coordination, quality, and efficiency of healthcare services. The ACA contains 20 initial ideas ranging from using geriatric assessments for care coordination to moving payment systems away from fee for service to salary models to state-based all-payer systems.

Creative healthcare leaders should consider submitting delivery system innovations to the CMI for possible pilot projects.

Independent Payment Advisory Board

In stark contrast to the creativity and intricate changes supported by the CMI, the blunt tool of cost control is enacted in §3403 with the creation of the Independent Payment Advisory Board. Its purpose is to reduce the per capita rate of growth in Medicare spending to the per capita gross domestic product plus one percentage point by 2018. Its recommendations become Medicare policy unless changed by Congress.

The 15-member independent panel to be appointed by the president and confirmed by the Senate will likely be composed of talented healthcare and policy professionals but is strictly limited in what it can recommend and implement. For example, the board can't change cost sharing for covered Medicare services. The only policy tool available is to cut Medicare payment rates for providers starting in 2014 (hospitals are exempt until 2020).

Because this section of the ACA transfers significant policy power from Congress to the White House, change is likely. Chapter 10 examines this and a number of other features of the ACA that have a high probability of modification in the future.

SUMMARY

The second major theory of the ACA is that payment policy can provide incentives for providers to increase desired behaviors and improve outcomes. Payment policy can also be used to reduce unwanted behaviors.

Accountable care organizations and bundled payments provide positive financial incentives for providers. However, the ACA also imposes penalties for high rates of inpatient readmissions and hospital-acquired conditions. The ACA also contains a much expanded set of tools to fight fraud, including the expansion of the Recovery Audit Contractors program to Medicaid.

Future payment changes are enabled through the Center for Medicare and Medicaid Innovation. However, if the cost of Medicare continues to grow beyond inflation, the new Independent Payment Advisory Board can unilaterally reduce payments to providers.

ANNOTATED REFERENCES

Allen, G. 2007. "Medicare Fraud Acute in South Florida." National Public Radio report. [Online broadcast; originally broadcast 10/11/07.] www.npr.org/templates/story/story.php?storyId=15178883

Blendon, R. J., M. Brodie, J. M. Benson, D. E. Altman, L. Levitt, T. Hoff, and L. Hugick. 1998. "Understanding the Managed Care Backlash." *Health Affairs* 17 (4): 80.

   Abstract: This paper examines the depth and breadth of the public backlash against managed care and the reasons for it. We conclude that the backlash is real and influenced by at least two principal factors: (1) A significant proportion of Americans report problems with managed care plans; and (2) the public perceives threatening and dramatic events in managed care that have been experienced by just a few. In addition, public concern is driven by fear that regardless of how well their plans perform today, care might not be available or paid for when they are very sick.

Bodenheimer, T., and H. H. Pham. 2010. "Primary Care: Current Problems and Proposed Solutions." *Health Affairs* 29 (5): 799.

CMS. 2011. "Details for Medicare Acute Care Episode Demonstration." [Online information; retrieved 1/10/11.] www.cms.gov/DemoProjectsEvalRpts/MD/itemdetail.asp?filterType= none&filterByDID=-99&sortByDID=3&sortOrder=descending&itemID= CMS1204388&intNumPerPage=10

> The Acute Care Episode (ACE) Demonstration provides global payments for acute care episodes within Medicare fee-for-service (FFS). The focus is on select orthopedic and cardiovascular inpatient procedures. ACE Demonstration goals are to improve quality for FFS Medicare beneficiaries; produce savings for providers, beneficiaries, and Medicare using market-based mechanisms; improve price and quality transparency for improved decision making; and increase collaboration among providers.

————. 2008. "The Medicare Recovery Audit Contractor (RAC) Program: An Evaluation of the 3-Year Demonstration." [Online report; published June 2008.] www.cms.gov/RAC/ Downloads/RACEvaluationReport.pdf

CMS/Office of Legislation. 2011. "Medicare 'Accountable Care Organizations' Shared Savings Program—New Section 1899 of Title XVIII. Preliminary Questions and Answers." [Online white paper; retrieved 1/10/11.] www.cms.gov/OfficeofLegislation/Downloads/ AccountableCareOrganization.pdf

> See the companion website for continuing updates (ache.org/books/reform).

Fisher, E. S., M. B. McClellan, J. Bertko, S. M. Lieberman, J. J. Lee, J. L. Lewis, and J. S. Skinner. 2009. "Fostering Accountable Health Care: Moving Forward in Medicare." *Health Affairs* 28 (2): w219.

Laxminarayan, R. 2010. "Avoiding the Unnecessary Costs of Hospital-Acquired Infections." [Online article; published 3/19/11.] www.rff.org/Publications/WPC/Pages/Avoiding-the- Unnecessary-Costs-of-Hospital-Acquired-Infections.aspx

Lohr, S. 2008. "Health Care That Puts a Computer on the Team." *New York Times* [Online article; published 12/26/08.] www.nytimes.com/2008/12/27/business/27record.html? pagewanted=1&_r=2&sq=Marshfield clinic&st=cse&scp=1

Mass.gov. 2011. "Healthcare Cost and Quality Council." [Online source; retrieved 1/10/11.] www.mass.gov/?pageID=hqcchomepage&L=1&L0=Home&sid=Ihqcc

> A state-based organization that publicly reports healthcare quality.

Medicare Payment Advisory Commission (MedPAC). 2009. Report to Congress, Chapter 2, p. 49, June.

————. 2007. Report to Congress, Chapter 5, June.

MN Community Measurement. 2011. Website. [Online source; retrieved 1/10/11.] www.mncm.org/site

> A state-based organization that publicly reports healthcare quality.

My San Antonio. 2009. "Providers Nationwide Watch Medicare Experiment Here." [Online article; published 10/12/09.] www.mysanantonio.com/default/article/Providers-nationwide- watch-Medicare-experiment-844486.php#page-1

Praxel, T. A. 2009. "Quality Improvement in the Marshfield Clinic." Presentation at the Institute for Clinical Systems Improvement Annual Meeting, Oct. 26.

Thorpe, K. E., and L. L. Ogden. 2010. "Analysis & Commentary: The Foundation That Health Reform Lays for Improved Payment, Care Coordination, and Prevention." *Health Affairs* 29 (6): 1183.

Wisconsin Collaborative for Healthcare Quality. 2011. Website. [Online source; retrieved 1/10/11.] www.wchq.org

A state-based organization that publicly reports healthcare quality.

CHAPTER 6

The Safety Net

ONE OF THE major policy problems addressed by the ACA is the lack of health insurance for more than 40 million Americans. However, lack of insurance does not always mean individuals go without healthcare. Many services are provided by the nation's safety net—public hospitals,[1] rural hospitals, and community health centers. For years, safety-net organizations have filled important roles, including providing:

- care to those without insurance;
- extensive training for physicians and other healthcare professionals;
- services that are culturally competent to the many unique communities throughout the nation; and
- services to those who live in rural communities.

Because safety-net providers receive a high percentage of their revenue from government sources, payment policies have been used to promote specific behaviors. For example, federally funded community health centers need to have independent community-based boards, and these boards must be composed mostly of consumers. Another example is the special payments made to some hospitals to provide for their uncompensated care, based on the percentage of Medicaid patients served.

Although the expansion of health insurance to almost all Americans may make the safety net less necessary in the future, the ACA contains many sections that support its continued success.

Eligibility

One of the most important strategies to increase access to health insurance is the expansion of the Medicaid program and the Children's Health Insurance Program (CHIP). This is contained in Title II: "Role of Public Programs." Improved access is accomplished by mandating a maximum income level (133 percent of the federal poverty level) to be used by every state for eligibility; such a policy also eliminates the many categories that Medicaid has historically used to determine eligibility. For example, single men were not covered under previous Medicaid policies.

One of the frustrating aspects of the Medicaid system over the years has been its close ties to cash assistance programs (i.e., welfare). Because of a concern that individuals were erroneously receiving cash assistance, most states implemented complex enrollment processes for both cash benefits and Medicaid. Unfortunately, this complexity deterred many individuals from enrolling. Researchers have estimated that in 2002, more than 60 percent of all uninsured children were eligible for public coverage, a figure that climbed to 74 percent in 2005 (Sommers 2007).

This problem is addressed in the ACA in §2201, which provides for simplification and coordination with online health insurance exchanges. In addition, §2202 permits hospitals to make presumptive eligibility determinations for Medicaid. This solves a long-standing problem—safety-net hospitals would provide emergency services, and because the patient had little incentive to apply later for Medicaid, the hospital would not be reimbursed.

These provisions in the ACA create an interesting challenge for safety-net providers. These new eligibility systems *should* decrease uncompensated care. However, the safety-net population has historically shown a reluctance to fully embrace new governmental programs, so these new policies may not be successful. In addition, the culture of complexity may not diminish if existing state government staff continue to administer the systems. Finally, individuals illegally present in the country will require services (usually in an emergency), and these will most likely be provided by the safety net.

In spite of these challenges, the ACA does anticipate the success of these simplified enrollment systems, and disproportionate share hospital payments should phase out (§2551) beginning in 2014.

Dual Eligible Beneficiaries

A unique aspect of the US health system is the diversity in its public payment systems. Medicare is managed by the federal government but also oversees each state-operated Medicaid program. Each state Medicaid system is unique, and many individuals are eligible for Medicare and Medicaid, leading to complex interactions between the payment systems. Coordination between programs is seen by many providers as problematic—particularly in the area of pharmaceuticals.

A new office to more effectively coordinate this care is established in §2602 and its goals are to ensure that dual eligible individuals receive all benefits to which they are entitled, to eliminate regulatory conflicts between rules of the Medicare and Medicaid programs, and to eliminate cost shifting between the Medicare and Medicaid programs and among related healthcare providers. Because this problem is finally acknowledged in the ACA, coordination likely will significantly improve in the future.

HOSPITALS

Chapter 5 discussed the new Center for Medicare and Medicaid Innovation. One demonstration in its list of potential projects is also specifically detailed in §2705—the Medicaid Global Payment System Demonstration Project. This project will "adjust the payments made to an eligible safety net hospital system or network from a fee-for-service payment structure to a global capitated payment model."

Global payment systems significantly reduce administrative costs for hospitals and doctors. A recent study of physician practices found that "12% of their net patient service revenue was used to cover the costs of excessive administrative complexity" (Blanchfield et al. 2010). If this demonstration succeeds it could lead to more global budgeting by other payers and significant administrative savings within the total healthcare system.

RURAL HEALTHCARE

The United States has a total resident population of more than 310 million, but the population is urbanized, with 82 percent residing in cities and suburbs as of 2008 (CIA 2011). Rural healthcare—particularly small rural hospitals—has been a payment policy target for federal officials for many years. (These providers are also helped that every state—regardless of population—has two senators.) The general policy direction has been to provide enough Medicare (and in some cases Medicaid) funding to rural hospitals for them to stay fiscally healthy, even if they are providing small volumes of care. The payment tool for this goal is cost-based reimbursement as opposed to the fixed payment prospective payment system used for most US hospitals. The most visible policy is the Medicare cost reimbursement for critical access hospitals that have fewer than 25 beds (CMS 2011a; Rural Assistance Center 2011a).

This policy agenda is expanded in the ACA. The ACA re-institutes reasonable cost payment for outpatient clinical lab tests performed by hospitals with fewer than 50 beds in qualified rural areas (§3122).

CMS will extend the Rural Community Hospital Demonstration for five years and expand the number of hospitals to 30 (§3123). For this demonstration, hospitals have to be located in one of the ten most sparsely populated states: Alaska, Idaho, Montana, Nebraska, Nevada, New Mexico, North Dakota, South Dakota, Utah, or Wyoming. Hospitals selected for participation in the demonstration will receive enough reimbursement to cover reasonable costs for covered inpatient services.

The Medicare wage index is a complex set of rules that uses average wages of healthcare workers in an area to calibrate DRG payment by MSA (metropolitan statistical area) and state. In 2011, the ACA (§10324) requires that hospitals located in "frontier states" that are paid with the DRG system have a wage index of at least 1.0 (if their index is already over 1.0 they keep this higher number). A frontier state is a state where at least 50 percent of its counties have a population density of less than six persons per square mile. CMS determined that the following states are frontier states: Montana, Wyoming, North Dakota, Nevada, and South Dakota. This designation moves the DRG payment rates in these states closer to the national average.

The rural and safety-net hospital demonstrations in the ACA are rarely discussed, and yet the cost-based emphasis in rural healthcare and the global payment system for safety-net hospitals might be the future models for hospital payment, as they can significantly reduce administrative costs.

COMMUNITY CLINICS

The third strand in the safety net is the growing list of community clinics. At the end of 2010, more than 1,000 federally qualified health centers (FQHCs) existed (CMS 2011b; Rural Assistance Center 2011b). Because community clinics are connected to their local neighborhoods, they have been popular with Democratic and Republican officials. This fondness continues in the ACA with significant funding increases in §5601 for FQHCs.

Section §5602 improves the methodology and criteria for designating medically underserved populations and health professions shortage areas.

This improvement is critical to community clinics as they recruit physicians and other heath professionals. This program offers health professionals federal subsidies of up to $145,000 for their education. In return, these professionals must practice in an underserved area for some portion of their careers. If they practice in underserved areas for six years, this debt is completely forgiven (HHS 2011).

SUMMARY

An important aspect of healthcare in the United States is the set of providers that comprise the safety net: public hospitals, rural providers, and community clinics. The ACA supports the continuation of their role through improved eligibility systems for Medicaid and CHIP and better coordination between Medicare and Medicaid.

The ACA provides substantial increases in funding for federally qualified health centers and improves rural hospital reimbursement. In addition, the law contains a new demonstration project for safety-net hospital global budgeting and a continuation of the rural demonstration project.

NOTE

1. The term "public hospital" continues to be used for large urban hospitals that serve the safety net mission. Most of these institutions began as local governmental units but have converted to some type of nonprofit status with nongovernmental governance.

ANNOTATED REFERENCES

Blanchfield, B. B., J. L. Heffernan, B. Osgood, R. R. Sheehan, and G. S. Meyer. 2010. "Saving Billions of Dollars—and Physicians' Time—by Streamlining Billing Practices." *Health Affairs* 29 (6): 1248.

Central Intelligence Agency (CIA). 2011. "CIA World Fact Book." [Online publication; retrieved 1/22/11.] www.cia.gov/library/publications/the-world-factbook/geos/us.html

CMS. 2011a. "Critical Access Hospitals." [Online information; retrieved 1/10/11.] www.cms.gov/CertificationandComplianc/04_CAHs.asp

———. 2011b. "Federally Qualified Health Center (FQHC)." [Online information; retrieved 1/10/11.] www.cms.gov/center/fqhc.asp

Rural Assistance Center. 2011a. "Critical Access Hospitals." [Online information; retrieved 1/10/11.] www.raconline.org/info_guides/hospitals/cah.php

———. 2011b. "Federally Qualified Health Centers." [Online information; retrieved 1/10/11.] www.raconline.org/info_guides/clinics/fqhc.php

Sommers, B. D. 2007. "Why Millions of Children Eligible for Medicaid and SCHIP are Uninsured: Poor Retention Versus Poor Take-Up." *Health Affairs* 26 (5): w560.

US Department of Health and Human Services (HHS). 2011. "National Health Services Corps." [Online information; retrieved 1/10/11.] http://nhsc.hrsa.gov/

> The NHSC is a network of 7,500 primary healthcare professionals and 10,000 sites as of September 30, 2010, working in underserved communities across the country. To support their service, the NHSC provides clinicians with financial support in the form of loan repayment and scholarships.

CHAPTER 7

Funds Flow Scenarios

THE FUNDS FLOW and incentives theory discussed in the introduction and chapters 5 and 6 also contains many uncertainties. Once again scenario planning can be used as an aid to strategy formulation. This chapter explores two issues that are tightly connected to the funds flow theory. Multiple scenarios are created, and strategy options are tested against each scenario to determine which options are most likely to succeed.

HEALTHCARE INFLATION

Health Cost Drivers and Physician Engagement

A key challenge in the US health system is to "bend the cost curve." The eventual goal is to reduce the rate of healthcare inflation to the growth in the economy. Success in meeting this goal would have these results:

- Health insurance becomes more affordable for employers and individuals.
- Pressures on the federal deficit are reduced.
- Medicare and Medicaid remain financially viable.
- US companies become more globally competitive because of reduced health benefit expenses.

However, many have criticized the ACA for not having enough strong policies to reduce healthcare inflation. The preceding chapters have outlined the many systems and incentives in the ACA that are focused on the goal of cost reduction. However, two major forces may determine healthcare inflation in the future.

The first uncertainty is intrinsic healthcare cost drivers. Cost drivers have two parts—price and frequency. If new technologies are developed that substantially improve patient care, they will be used. If these technologies are expensive, this cost will contribute to inflation. On the other hand, value-based purchasing may hold down inflation. An example of value-based purchasing is when drug companies introduce generic pharmaceuticals that have clinical efficacy similar to brand-name drugs but which cost less.

The second uncertainty is physician engagement. Many of the policies in the ACA are designed to encourage "systems-based care." However, most of the medical practices in the United States are small (Liebhaber and Grossman 2007) and their willingness to become larger or affiliate with hospitals is unknown. True cost management success with ACOs and bundled payments requires active and engaged physicians.

The scenario cross for these two uncertain trends is displayed in Exhibit 7.1.

Scenarios

1. Global Budgets

Healthcare technology continues to improve and become more expensive. Although some physician practices have integrated with hospitals, most specialists remain independent and in small groups. As a result, engaging physicians in ACOs and bundled payment projects is difficult. In addition, the fee-for-service system continues to be the dominant payment methodology and the number and range of services being billed expands dramatically. Because of the resulting inflation, the federal government enacts new legislation that requires global budgets for all hospitals that are negotiated annually with each state's health department. An SGR (sustainable growth rate)–type physician payment system is implemented in Medicare, Medicaid, and all private insurance.

2. Staying Alive

Although many new technologies are being brought to market, physicians are actively engaged with hospitals in new relationships. These include direct employment, professional service agreements, or active participation in ACOs. These integrated organizations help bring the new technologies carefully into use. In addition, physicians work closely with hospital staff to review older technologies and processes to identify savings. The result is a marked improvement in patient care with adequate financial performance for hospitals and physicians.

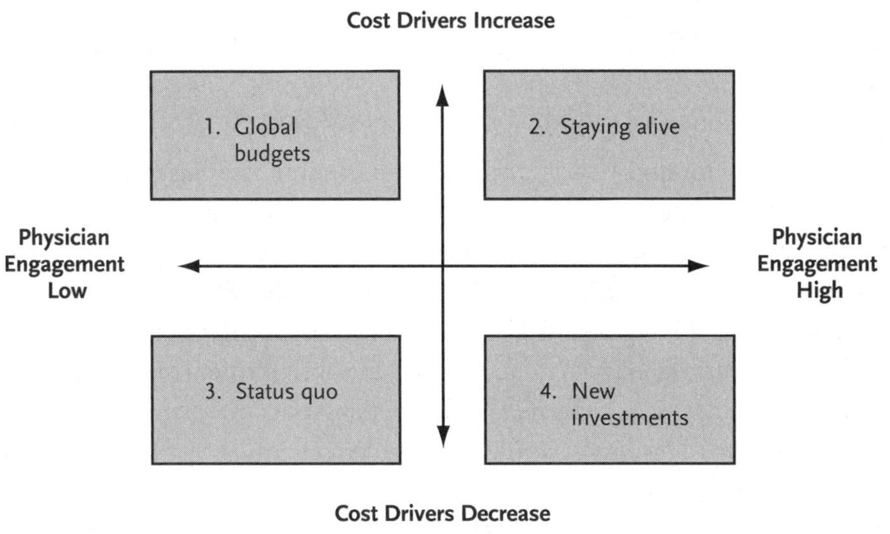

Exhibit 7.1
Scenario Cross
for Healthcare
Inflation

Cost Drivers Increase

1. Global
budgets

2. Staying alive

Physician
Engagement
Low

Physician
Engagement
High

3. Status quo

4. New
investments

Cost Drivers Decrease

3. Status Quo

Although healthcare technology inflation is low, engaging physicians in any of the new payment models now available in the ACA is difficult. Hospitals understand the missed opportunities and begin a few highly selective programs to accept bundled payments. They avoid ACOs until they have better relationships with their physicians. Healthcare inflation continues slightly higher than the growth of the gross domestic product (GDP).

4. New Investments

Vendors of devices and drugs provide "value solutions" to clinical challenges. Physicians sit on the hospital's side of the table when negotiating with vendors. In addition, physicians participate actively with hospital staff to review older technology and update treatment protocols based on the results of comparative effectiveness research. All new types of payment models (e.g., ACOs, bundled payments) are embraced. Healthcare inflation is reduced to the level of the general inflation. Hospital financial results are vastly improved and new investments in facilities, research, and community outreach are made.

Strategy Options

The challenge of healthcare inflation can be met with a number of organizational strategies. Most strategies will be led by hospitals, but physicians and health plans are also likely to develop new structures to meet this challenge and opportunity.

1. Hospital and Physicians Form a Fully Integrated System

A clear option for hospitals, physicians, and in some cases health plans is to become a fully integrated system (e.g., Geisinger in Pennsylvania, Denver Health, Cleveland Clinic). This structure is well suited to all scenarios except 3, status quo. Although physicians are not highly engaged in scenario 1, the structure of integrated systems allows the management systems to succeed in the cost-challenged environment. However, forming these large systems is difficult, which is reflected by the small number of these organizations operating today. This makes implementing this strategy difficult.

2. Hospitals Develop ACOs and Mechanisms to Accept Bundled Payments

A less intense integration option is for a hospital and its physicians to form an accountable care organization. Chapter 5 reviewed a number of structural options that can be used to construct the ACO. Once the ACO structure is implemented, using this structure and relationship to engage in accepting bundled payments is relatively straightforward.

The ACO model is highly dependent on physician engagement and therefore works well for scenarios 2 and 4, with the financial results better in scenario 4.

3. Physicians Develop ACOs and Mechanisms to Accept Bundled Payments

Because the majority of the primary care physicians in the United States are now employed by hospitals (Crosson and Tollen 2010), hospitals may seem the logical hub for creating ACOs. However, many effective care delivery systems have begun as medical practices that later acquired hospitals and health plans (e.g., Kaiser Permanente). Therefore, in some communities physicians may band together to form ACOs to maintain physician leadership and control. These physician-led ACOs would contract for hospital services and in some cases would also begin to accept bundled payments. The ACA envisioned this possibility by allowing many legal structures to be used to form ACOs. This strategy works well with scenarios 2 and 4 and could also work well with scenario 1 if the hospitals could contract back to the ACO to help them maintain efficient operations.

4. Physicians Partner with Health Plans

Although the chronic disease management and primary care systems discussed in Chapter 1 are key to succeeding in a shared savings environment, many other skills are also required. One of these is longitudinal analysis of patient claims data, a skill that most physician practices lack; health plans, however, are skilled at this task and many others that are required for ACOs to succeed. Therefore, physicians may choose to partner with health plans rather than hospitals.

An interesting example of a precursor of this strategy can be seen in UnitedHealth subsidiary Ingenix's acquisition of Axolotl, which provides interoperable exchange of clinic information and is used by nearly 30,000 physicians, 100,000 healthcare professionals, 20 regional health information organizations (RHIOs), and four statewide health information exchanges. This system provides clinical data interchange services for more than 35 million patients (UnitedHealth Group 2010). By becoming a clinical data partner with providers, UnitedHealth will move into a relationship that goes beyond simply paying claims.

This strategy would work well for scenarios 2 and 4 and scenario 3, as the status quo environment will present new opportunities for innovation. However, the strategy will not succeed in scenario 1 as it lacks a strong connection to hospitals.

Additional strategy options can be found at the companion website at ache.org/books/reform.

SAFETY-NET SUCCESS

Community Engagement Versus Increased Medicaid Eligibility

The ACA provides a number of policies to strengthen the safety net: public hospitals, rural healthcare, and community clinics (see Chapter 6). It also includes a number of strategies to increase enrollment in two major public programs: Medicaid and CHIP. The success of these improved eligibility systems is uncertain and therefore this policy forms one arm of the strategy cross.

A second major uncertainty for the safety net is safety-net providers' level of community engagement. One major role for the safety net has been to provide uncompensated care, and the need for this will diminish after the ACA is fully implemented. For these institutions to succeed, they will need to be engaged with their unique communities (e.g., special needs, cultural, academic) to demonstrate that they have a mission that is significantly different from the balance of the delivery system. How well they will accomplish this goal is uncertain. Exhibit 7.2 illustrates the scenario cross for Medicaid eligibility and community engagement.

**Exhibit 7.2
Scenario Cross
for Medicaid
Eligibility and
Community
Engagement**

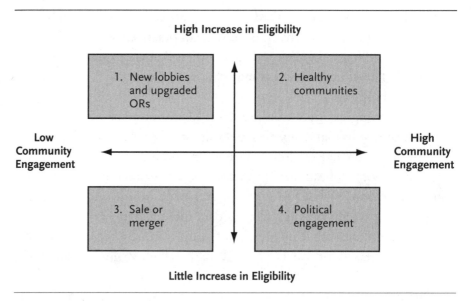

Scenarios

1. New Lobbies and Upgraded Operating Rooms

Safety-net providers realize increased net revenues as a result of decreased uncompensated care. However, they are unsuccessful in engaging their core communities and decide to compete aggressively to attract new patients that have historically gone to non–safety-net providers. They use their new funds to upgrade facilities and equipment with a particular emphasis on patient amenities.

2. Healthy Communities

New net revenues resulting from decreased uncompensated care are realized and directed toward a number of healthy-community initiatives such as new farmers markets and a partnership with the schools to increase physical fitness. An ACO is formed for Medicaid patients and easily meets its financial targets because of the improving health status of the community it serves.

3. Sale or Merger

Improved eligibility systems are poorly implemented and safety-net providers do not see improved net revenues. In addition, the community thinks the hospitals have achieved this new funding stream and provides little engagement or support. Safety-net providers seek new partners for merger. If merger is not possible, they close and sell the real estate. The closing of St. Vincent's in New York City is an example of this scenario (Otterman 2010).

4. Political Engagement

Although hoped-for new Medicaid revenues have not occurred, the communities that are engaged with safety-net providers continue to provide strong support and engagement. These communities lead a community organizing campaign to modify state and federal statutes, regulations, and rules to ensure that the goals of increased Medicaid and CHIP enrollment are met.

Strategy Options

1. Become Part of a Bigger Structure

Safety-net providers have historically been independent organizations. However, because the ACA rewards system-based care, alignment or affiliation with larger structures may be wise. At the minimum, providers should participate in or sponsor ACOs. This strategy is particularly important for scenarios 3 and 4.

2. Broaden the Array of Services

Safety-net providers have frequently offered services unique to their organizations (e.g., on-site interpreters). More nontraditional services could be added, for example, alternative and complementary medicine or social services. This strategy would be effective in scenarios 2 and 4.

3. Work with Small Employers

Many of the patients of safety-net providers work for small employers. In 2014, these individuals will have health insurance but will still have loyalties to the safety net. This relationship could be enhanced if the providers offer work-site wellness programs and ACO-type programs for small employers. This works well for scenarios 1 and 2.

4. Rejoin Government

Becoming part of local government again and benefiting from the ability to receive direct tax-based funding may be unthinkable for some providers who have carefully disentangled themselves from their local or state government. However, scenario 3 predicts a gloomy future, and this may be the only acceptable strategy to maintain needed community services.

Additional strategy options can be found at the companion website at ache.org/books/reform.

SUMMARY

The healthcare inflation scenarios contain two major uncertainties: physician engagement and internal cost drivers. Potential strategies for this future include the following

1. hospitals and physicians form fully integrated systems,
2. hospitals develop ACOs and mechanisms to accept bundled payments,
3. physicians develop ACOs and mechanisms to accept bundled payments, and
4. physicians partner with health plans.

The safety-net success scenarios contain two major uncertainties: Medicaid eligibility and community engagement. Potential future strategies are to

1. become part of a bigger structure,
2. broaden the array of services,
3. work with small employers, and
4. rejoin government.

ANNOTATED REFERENCES

Crosson, F. J., and L. A. Tollen. 2010. *Partners in Health: How Physicians and Hospitals Can Be Accountable Together*, 31. San Francisco: Jossey-Bass.

Liebhaber, A., and J. M. Grossman. 2007. "Physicians Moving to Mid-sized, Single-Specialty Practices: Tracking Report No. 18." [Online report; published Aug. 2007.] www.hschange.com/CONTENT/941/

> In 1996–97 the number of solo/two-physician practices was 40.7 percent of the total physician workforce. This number declined to 37.4 percent in 1998–99, 35.2 percent in 2000–01, and 32.5 percent in 2004–05. Practices of three to five physicians were 12.5 percent of the total in 1996–97, 9.6 percent in 1998–99, 11.7 percent in 2000–01, and back down to 9.8 percent in 2004–05. Groups of 6 to 50 were 13.1 percent of the total in 1996–97, 14.2 percent in 1998–99, 15.8 percent in 2000–01, and rising to 17.6 percent in 2004–05. In total, in 2004–05, 59.9 percent of physicians were practicing in groups of 50 or less in the United States.

Otterman, S. 2010. "St. Vincent's Votes to Shut Hospital in Manhattan." *The New York Times*. [Online article; published 5/6/2010.] www.nytimes.com/2010/04/07/nyregion/07vincents.html?_r=1

UnitedHealth Group. 2010. "Ingenix and Axolotl to Combine." [Online press release; published 8/16/10.] www.unitedhealthgroup.com/newsroom/news.aspx?id= 08e3bd40-2176-4f0f-bbca-f74fa75087f6

> "Ingenix, a leading health information technology and services company, today announced it is acquiring Axolotl, a leading provider of health information exchange (HIE) services. The combined company will enable health information to be shared effectively and securely for the benefit of patients and healthcare professionals. The Axolotl management team will remain in place and will lead Ingenix's efforts in healthcare community connectivity."

PART 3

Markets

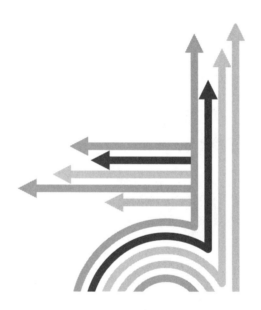

CHAPTER 8

The Perfect Market:
Health Insurance Reform

THE CURRENT VERSION of the US Pledge of Allegiance reads, "I pledge allegiance to the flag of the United States of America, and to the republic for which it stands, one nation under God, indivisible, with *liberty and justice for all.*" "Liberty and justice for all" summarizes the conflicting values in the US government that have been present since its founding. *Liberty:* we are on our own to succeed or fail; therefore keep the government off my back. *Justice for all:* we are all in this together; government is a tool to advance the common good.

The final theory of the ACA is based in liberty and the force of the free market to optimize healthcare costs and value. The introduction of this book provides an overview of the markets theory as applied to healthcare, and this chapter explores some of the market-based policies in the ACA that will shape US healthcare in the future.

Throughout the debate surrounding the ACA, the title of the legislation vacillated between "health reform" and "health insurance reform." The final product does make substantial changes to the health insurance system, and the details are too numerous to be analyzed in this book. However, three key policies in the new health insurance system will affect providers significantly and should be considered by healthcare leaders as they develop strategic plans. These policies are key elements in the markets theory of the ACA and are based on some of the best practices in the health insurance industry. The policies are universal coverage, standard benefits, and increased government regulation to maintain a fair playing field.

UNIVERSAL COVERAGE

Many problems prompted healthcare reform. However, the strongest force was the increasing population of uninsured with concomitant untreated illnesses and financial disasters. Hence, the most prominent feature of the ACA is its multiple mechanisms to increase the rate of health insurance.

The problem of the lack of insurance is illustrated by a study of individuals with chronic conditions who were undiagnosed or inadequately treated (Exhibit 8.1) (Wilper et al. 2009).

Wilper and colleagues conclude in their study, "Gaining insurance and a diagnosis might not guarantee optimal treatment of chronic conditions, unless these achievements are coupled with other system improvements such as expanded access to primary and preventive care, reducing financial barriers to care, and a focus on chronic disease management in lieu of the current episodic care model."

Fortunately, the expansion of coverage is a principal goal of the ACA. Eibner and colleagues at RAND have developed simulation models that predict that 94.6 percent of US workers will be covered by comprehensive health insurance once the ACA is fully implemented (Eibner, Hussey, and Girosi 2010).

Universal coverage promotes a stable and competitive market and eliminates the need for many of the worst practices of the health insurance system—for example, rating or exclusions for preexisting conditions. In addition, universal coverage provides prevention, early treatment, and chronic disease management—all of which have been demonstrated to improve quality and decrease costs (see chapters 1 and 3).

Another benefit of universal and portable coverage is its support of innovation and enterprise. If an inventor has a preexisting condition, she may choose to remain with her current employer to keep her health insurance. However, after the implementation of the ACA, this "job lock" is eliminated and the inventor can start her own company and still retain affordable health insurance.

The sections of the ACA that drive this expanded coverage are contained in Title I: "Quality, Affordable Health Care for all Americans" and Title II: "Role of Public Programs" (see Chapter 6).

BENEFITS

A primary tool to meet the goals of the ACA is the state-based health insurance exchange (HIE), which will provide a convenient website through which individuals and employees of small firms can enroll in the health

Exhibit 8.1
Effect of Lack
of Insurance
on Chronic
Disease Care:
Undiagnosed
and Uncontrolled
Diabetes,
Hypertension,
and Elevated
Cholesterol
Among US
Adults
Ages 18–64,
by Insurance
Status, Predictive
Margins

Condition	Insured	Uninsured	p value
Diabetes mellitus			
Undiagnosed[a]	23.2%	46.0%	0.001
Uncontrolled[b]	44.2	46.6	0.70
Hypertension			
Undiagnosed	23.7	26.3	0.26
Uncontrolled[c]	51.4	58.3	0.02
Elevated cholesterol[d]			
Undiagnosed	29.9	52.1	<0.001
Uncontrolled	60.4	77.5	<0.001

Based on authors' analysis of National Health and Nutrition Examination Survey data.

Notes: Adjusted for age, sex, race/ethnicity, and income. A version of this exhibit showing 95 percent confidence intervals is available as Supplemental Exhibit 3 in the Technical Appendix, online at http://content.healthaffairs.org/cgi/content/full/hlthaff.28.6.w1151/DC2.

[a]Defined as fasting plasma glucose greater than 126mg/dl, with no previous diabetes.

[b]Defined as HbA1c greater than 7.0 percent.

[c]Defined as average blood pressure greater than 140/90.

[d]Based on National Cholesterol Education Panel Adult Treatment Panel II (ATP II) guidelines. Lab diagnosis excludes people with triglyceride levels greater than 400 mg/dl. Repeat analysis using concurrent cholesterol guidelines did not alter these results.

Source: Used with permission from Project Hope/*Health Affairs* Journal, from "Hypertension, Diabetes, and Elevated Cholesterol among Insured and Uninsured U.S. Adults" by A. P. Wilper, S. Woolhandler, K. E. Lasser, D. McCormick, D. H. Bor, and D. U. Himmelstein. 2009. *Health Affairs* 28 (6): w1151; permission conveyed through Copyright Clearance Center, Inc.

plan of their choice. An HIE will also help individuals estimate the level of subsidy they will receive from the federal government to purchase this insurance. HIEs are designed to emulate the Health Connector in Massachusetts, which substantially increased coverage. The Massachusetts Health Connector (2011) reports that:

> Estimates of how many uninsured there were in Massachusetts when the landmark legislation was signed into law on April 12, 2006, range from 400,000 to 650,000. For tax year 2008, over 95% of tax filers were insured for the full year while 96.4% were insured at some point during the year, according to the Massachusetts Department of Revenue. Only 53,000 were subject to the tax penalty while another 50,000 uninsured were not penalized because they could not afford to buy it or because of their religious beliefs.

The funds for the subsidies in the new federal health insurance exchanges come from reduced Medicare payment to providers and a variety of new taxes.

To be effective, the HIEs need to ensure that each participating health plan has comparable products. The ACA accomplishes this through two mechanisms: standard benefits and a standard method to calculate premiums. Standardization promotes fair market competition and is a key to the success of the markets theory of the ACA.

Benefit design in health insurance has always been controversial, with extended debates on coverage for mental health and substance abuse, disease specific plans, and plans with such high deductibles as to be equivalent to no insurance. The benefit design question is left to HHS (§1302) but must include "at least the following general categories and the items and services covered within the categories:

1. ambulatory patient services;
2. emergency services;
3. hospitalization;
4. maternity and newborn care;
5. mental health and substance use disorder services, including behavioral health treatment;
6. prescription drugs;
7. rehabilitative and habilitative services and devices;
8. laboratory services;
9. preventive and wellness services and chronic disease management; and
10. pediatric services, including oral and vision care."

HHS is charged with surveying large employer group insurance benefits designs to ensure that the benefits included in insurance sold on the HIE are consistent. In addition, the ACA (§1201) also provides that coverage must be extended to individuals participating in clinical trials. Historically a number of types of providers (e.g., chiropracters, acupuncturists) have been excluded from employer-sponsored insurance. Although they are now included in some companies' benefits sets, inclusion is not yet uniform. Therefore, after the initial benefit set is determined by HHS, intense lobbying for inclusion by those provider groups left out will likely ensue. The other method of standardization is to only permit four types of policies to be sold with varying levels of coinsurance and deductibles (§1302). The cost of each plan is based on the insurance companies' actuarial cost of all of the benefits that are determined by HHS; therefore each insurance company will calculate the average cost of its policy for ambulatory patient services, emergency services, hospitalizations, and so forth (see list above). This cost is then considered the 100 percent cost for health insurance provided by this insurance company.

Consumers will be able to choose varying levels of coinsurance and copays for the insurance company policy they select. The policy with the lowest monthly premium is the bronze level; this provides a level of coverage that is designed to provide benefits that are actuarially equivalent to 60 percent of the full actuarial value of the benefits. Other levels include silver (70 percent), gold (80 percent), and platinum (90 percent).

The markets theory of the ACA predicts that these two standardizations will promote price competition by health plans and a general reduction in the growth of healthcare costs.

INCREASED GOVERNMENT REGULATION

The HIE should promote aggressive competition between health plans, which does not currently exist. In fact, critics have asserted that in some geographic areas health plans practice shadow pricing, where all competitors' prices in the area rise at approximately the same rate.

In a study from 2001 to 2003, Chollet and Liu (2005) examined 52 insurers in three contiguous jurisdictions: Maryland, Virginia, and the District of Columbia. They found that "monopolistic pricing was observed among the largest insurers and could be measured against the pricing behavior of mid-sized insurers in the market. In addition, shadow pricing by the smallest insurers in the market was observed, even controlling for potential diseconomies of scale associated with small size."

Medical Loss Ratios

The ACA mandates that insurance sold in the United States have medical loss ratios (MLRs) of 85 percent for large employers and 80 percent for small employers (§1001.) The medical loss ratio is the percentage of the revenue a health plan receives that is spent on healthcare services. The regulations surrounding this section are complex and HHS has worked closely with the National Association of Insurance Commissioners to develop them.

The effects of MLR rules may be unpredictable. Some smaller insurance companies that are focused on the individual market may be unable to meet these rules and may cease to exist. Some services that were provided directly by health plans (e.g., disease management) may be subcontracted back to providers to meet the MLR.

Rate Increases

One of the intense issues preceding the enactment of the ACA was the large rate increases for individuals in some markets. Some have speculated that the 39 percent increase proposed by WellPoint in California helped keep the legislation alive (Grier 2010).

The ACA addressed this issue in §1003, "Ensuring that Consumers Get Value for Their Dollars." This section provides for a review of rate increases each year by the states and the federal government and possible exclusion of health plans whose rate increases are too large. Some states already have rate approval authority, and the coordination of these policies will require intricate regulations.

Administrative Simplification

The high administrative costs of the US health system are addressed in §1104. The section provides a mechanism to create a single set of "operating rules" for each financial transaction between health plans and providers. It builds on the regulations contained in the Health Insurance Portability and Accountability Act of 1996. In addition to standards for electronic transactions, the section includes improvements to unravel much of the complexity of the current system, such as

- determining an individual's eligibility and financial responsibility for specific services prior to or at the point of care;
- requiring minimal augmentation of electronic systems by paper or other communications; and
- providing for timely acknowledgment, response, and status reporting that supports a transparent claims and denial management process.

This work coincides with the expansion of HIT into medical practices. Hopefully this new clinical automation will coincide with the adoption of the new standardized operating rules, and much of today's complex paper systems will be eliminated.

A True Marketplace?

Although the HIEs are designed to support the markets theory in the ACA, innovation will be difficult for health plans. The standard benefit set will restrict some creativity in benefit design and the MLR requirement would not be required in a functioning market.

However, the large populations that will buy their insurance through exchanges will provide new opportunities to create national products—in insurance and in provider systems. These possible future scenarios are explored in Chapter 9.

SUMMARY

The third major theory of the ACA is that a competitive marketplace will deliver value in costs and quality. The new state-based health insurance exchanges are the most visible portion of the ACA that supports this theory.

Estimates predict that when the ACA is fully implemented, 94.6 percent of Americans will have health insurance as a result of the HIEs and the mandate to have health insurance. The new market for health insurance in the HIEs is made competitive by standardized healthcare benefits and four levels of deductibles and coinsurance.

The ACA adds new rules for the health insurance market, including mandatory medical loss ratios and a rate increase review process. The ACA has increased efforts to reduce costs in the health insurance system through administrative simplification of claims processing.

ANNOTATED REFERENCES

Chollet, D., and S. Liu. 2005. "The Elephants in Your Back Yard: Monopolistic Pricing in Health Insurance Markets." *Abstacts AcademyHealth Meeting* 22: (Abstract no. 3486).

Eibner, C., P. S. Hussey, and F. Girosi. 2010. "The Effects of the Affordable Care Act on Workers' Health Insurance Coverage." *New England Journal of Medicine* 363 (15): 1393–95.

Grier, P. 2010. "New Jolt for Healthcare Reform? Insurer Hikes Rates 39 Percent." *The Christian Science Monitor*. [Online article; published 2/11/10.] www.csmonitor.com/USA/Politics/2010/0211/New-Jolt-for-healthcare-reform-Insurer-hikes-rates-39-percent

Health Connector. 2011. "Health Reform Facts and Figures: Winter 2010/2011." [Online white paper; retrieved 1/24/11.] www.mahealthconnector.org/portal/binary/com.epicentric.contentmanagement.servlet.ContentDeliveryServlet/Health%2520Care%2520Reform/Facts%2520and%2520Figures/Facts%2520and%2520Figures.pdf

Wilper, A. P., S. Woolhandler, K. E. Lasser, D. McCormick, D. H. Bor, and D. U. Himmelstein. 2009. "Hypertension, Diabetes, and Elevated Cholesterol Among Insured and Uninsured U.S. Adults." *Health Affairs* 28 (6): w1151.

CHAPTER 9

Market Scenarios

THE MARKETS THEORY discussed in the introduction and Chapter 8 has the greatest level of uncertainty of the three theories of the ACA. Market forces have a limited history of success in reducing healthcare costs or improving quality. However, once again scenario planning can be used as an aid to strategy formulation. Two major trends are explored with the creation of multiple scenarios and strategy options.

NATIONAL MARKETS

Participation in Health Exchanges and Local/National Providers

A key feature of the ACA is the state-based health insurance exchange (HIE). HIEs are designed in the ACA to be used by individuals and employees of small businesses. One possible future is that they function more effectively than expected and larger employers seek to use them for their employees. For example, some employers may choose to pay the $2,000 fine per employee, increase their employees' salary, and let employees use the exchanges to buy insurance. Or, HHS may permit large employers to buy through the exchanges without penalty (§1001) to encourage competition among health plans. Employers will enjoy several advantages:

- They would no longer manage this benefit with staffing and resources (similar to the shift to defined contributions from retirement plans).

- Each employee could select a health plan that meets her specific needs.
- The HIEs would be regulated and therefore the employer would be assured that employees are receiving good coverage through a regulated insurance product.

The second important question is whether healthcare delivery markets will continue to be local or whether national organizations will emerge. Two organizations may be revealing the answer to this question. Kaiser Permanente operates integrated care systems in California, Colorado, Hawaii, Georgia, the Washington DC area, Oregon, Ohio, and Washington. Because of the experience Kaiser has gathered in these unique markets, expansion nationally may be relatively straightforward. Another more loosely structured model is the Mayo Health System, which is a family of clinics, hospitals, and other healthcare facilities serving 70 communities in Minnesota, Iowa, and Wisconsin. Patients receive healthcare at their local clinic or hospital and, when needed, receive specialized care at the Mayo Clinic in Rochester, Minnesota. Each year the system serves more than one million patients. This model also might be easily expanded nationally.

Mayo is currently testing many new e-health initiatives that can be used throughout the world to provide specialty consultation to primary care providers in their offices. This allows Mayo to expand its services geographically without the need to construct clinics and relocate physicans (LaRusso 2010).

The scenario cross for these two trends is displayed in Exhibit 9.1.

Scenarios

1. ACOs for All

Local providers organize and form ACOs for Medicare; however, they begin to accept partial capitation and become efficient in care delivery. They create insurance products and compete effectively against national insurance companies because of their lower cost.

Local providers also form specialty ACOs. Just as retailers segment markets and develop specific products to sell to these markets, local ACOs are developed that target niche markets. Some examples are partnerships with health clubs and spas for a physically fit ACO. Another ACO might be designed for residents of long-term-care facilities.

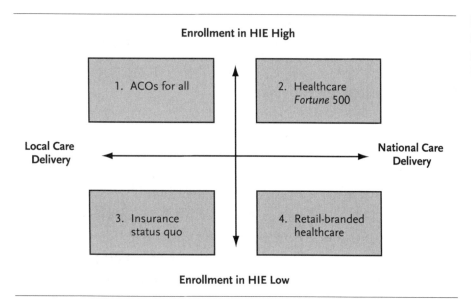

**Exhibit 9.1
Scenario Cross
for National
Markets**

2. Healthcare Fortune 500

Some large integrated providers take their brand and systems into new markets and acquire local doctors and hospitals. To finance this expansion they convert to for-profit status and become publicly held companies. They engage in aggressive advertising and, because of their efficient systems, compete effectively on price.

In response, the large national health plans acquire primary care practices to recapture market share.

3. Insurance Status Quo

Most of the health plans available in the HIE are plans in existence before the ACA. They make minor modifications to their benefit structures to conform to the HIE rules. They maintain their market shares but increase their enrollment from the individual and small-group market.

Providers create ACOs—but just for Medicare, and resist using them for other markets.

4. Retail-Branded Healthcare

Some large integrated providers take their brand and systems into new markets and provide care by forming relationships with local physicians and hospitals. However, they do not establish ACOs or insurance products. Their strategy to gain market share is to partner with retailers for store-based, full-service primary care clinics and refer some specialty care back to their home cities. This is a form of medical tourism within the United States.

Strategy Options for Providers

These strategy options are focused on hospitals, physician groups, and other direct providers of patient care.

1. Form a Local ACO

Hospitals and their medical staffs form ACOs—initially to care for Medicare patients. Once data systems and chronic disease management programs are in place and working well, the ACO accepts partial capitation. Once this succeeds, the ACO converts into a health plan and begins to compete in the HIE. This strategy is particularly effective for scenario 1 and may be needed to defend against strategies 2 and 4.

2. Joint Branding and Marketing with a National System

A hospital and its medical staff can enter into an agreement with a renowned national provider of care. This agreement would allow the provider to use the national player's care processes and data systems. The provider would also market itself under the brand of the national provider. This strategy would work well for scenario 2 and could lead to a merger with the national provider. It could also work well as a defensive strategy for scenario 4.

3. Merger with a National System

Local hospitals and doctors could be acquired by a national provider. This is scenario 2. However, hospital mergers have not always gone well, and mergers in the new environment may include providers who do not have a history of working well together. This scenario also includes developing an ACO and other insurance products, which adds a level of complexity.

Strategy Options for Health Plans

These strategy options are for health plans.

1. Joint Venture with Providers to Develop ACOs

Most hospitals and medical groups do not have the necessary data systems or care systems to start up and effectively manage an ACO. These systems can be purchased or created internally. Another option is for health plans and providers to create a joint venture to optimize each of the organization's strengths. This strategy would work well for all scenarios except 2.

2. Mine Data, Find Affinity Groups, and Create Expanded Products

Health plans have large databases and sophisticated analysts. They could use these resources to create products that go beyond health services. Large consumer databases are available, and the health plan could merge these data sources with their own systems. Data mining techniques could be used to discover affinity groups.

For example, data mining might reveal a group of seniors who like to travel. The health plan could develop a unique ACO product that would include travel arrangements and special coverage for health services while traveling. This would work well for scenarios 1 and 2.

3. Offer Clinical Services—Urgent Care, Primary Care, Disease Management

If providers develop effective ACOs that transform into health insurance products, traditional health plans will need a defensive strategy or will be forced out of the market. Therefore, a reasonable strategy is to provide health services such as urgent care, primary care, and disease management to enrollees. This is a good defensive strategy for scenario 1 and would work well on a national level with scenarios 2 and 4.

Additional strategy options can be found at the companion website at ache.org/books/reform.

SUMMARY

A set of scenarios based on the markets theory of the ACA can be created around the uncertainties of enrollment in health insurance exchanges and the question of whether healthcare provider and insurance markets remain locally oriented or become national.

Three strategies for *providers* are suggested:

1. Form a local ACO.
2. Engage in joint branding and marketing with a national system.
3. Merge with a national system.

Three strategies for *health plans* are also suggested:

1. Joint venture with providers to develop ACOs.
2. Mine data, find affinity groups, and create expanded products.
3. Offer clinical services—urgent care, primary care, disease management.

REFERENCE

LaRusso, N. F. 2010. Presentation at the University of St. Thomas Executive Conference on the Future of Healthcare. Minneapolis, MN, Nov. 5.

PART 4

The Future

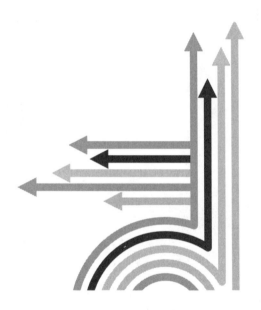

CHAPTER 10

The Future

"HEALTHCARE REFORM IS a journey—not a destination," says former US Senator Dave Durenberger, one of the architects of US health policy in the 1980s and 1990s. Every year, Congress (and each state legislature) revises existing laws to meet the current environment, so healthcare reform is never finished. Laws usually change because of

- legislation that works poorly or is difficult to implement;
- new policies that are working in pilots and demonstrations that can be applied more broadly;
- funding availability or lack thereof; or
- changes in the legislative majority party or the executive branch that bring a new governing philosophy.

This chapter explores the processes of change and identifies the sections of the ACA that might be modified and what is likely to remain. In addition, the major strategic themes that have appeared in the scenarios chapters are identified. The book concludes with an invitation for healthcare leaders to get involved in the policy process and some suggested steps to that end.

THE PROCESS

Because the enactment of the ACA was controversial and partisan, some change to the ACA is likely. The substantial gains by Republicans in the 2010 election almost guarantee changes. A number of strategies and tools can be used to change existing law.

Lawsuits

The most direct method to change legislation is with a lawsuit. More than 20 states have filed a lawsuit that challenges a portion of the ACA (§1501) that mandates that individuals maintain insurance coverage or pay a penalty. These states contend that by compelling individuals to buy goods or services and penalizing them if they do not, the ACA oversteps the power of the federal government under the Constitution's commerce clause. This clause authorizes the federal government to regulate interstate commerce; the states contend that the law punishes an individual for commercial *inactivity*.

The states add that the mandate encroaches on their sovereignty. The lawsuit argues that the ACA unfairly imposes significant new costs on state governments by expanding Medicaid eligibility to 133 percent of the federal poverty level. The question of the relative power of the federal government to impose mandates on individuals and states is beyond the scope of this book. However, numerous legal debates over the years have argued about the use of the commerce clause to expand federal power, and these lawsuits likely will reach the US Supreme Court and be decided there. This may occur before 2014, when the insurance mandate begins.

Oversight Hearings by Congress

Another possible way to change legislation is through congressional hearings and oversight. Administration officials can be called on to testify, and modifications may be made to regulations. Congress can threaten to reduce a federal agency's budget if it does not respond to recommendations from a committee.

New Legislation and Budget Changes

The most likely vehicle for change is new legislation. However, all changes need to be negotiated with the president, and President Obama would likely veto any radical change to the ACA. More likely, legislation will be created that corrects perceived errors in the ACA and reduces funding for some aspects of the law.

Because the House of Representatives proposes all appropriations, some key elements of the ACA might not receive funding. For example, the individual mandate enforcement is the responsibility of the Internal Revenue Service (IRS); if no new funds are appropriated to the IRS, this task may not be accomplished.

2012 Presidential Election

The next presidential election will clearly influence the full implementation of the ACA because the health insurance exchanges and insurance mandate begin in 2014. If President Obama runs and is defeated, substantial changes in the ACA could occur. However, much of the ACA was negotiated with the healthcare industry and was based on their recommendations, so wholesale changes are unlikely.

POTENTIAL TARGETS FOR CHANGE

Insurance Mandate

The section of the ACA that is most often seen as inconsistent with American values is the insurance mandate. This mandate will be subject to the change strategies outlined in the previous section. If this mandate is repealed, the ACA begins to unravel.

The most likely individuals to resist having coverage are the healthiest. If the healthy no longer buy insurance, rates for those left in the HIE will increase, fewer individuals will be able to afford health insurance, and eventually the system will collapse. (This is sometimes called the risk-pool death spiral.) In response to this inflation, health insurers will attempt to again use preexisting conditions to deny individuals coverage. Doctors and hospitals will provide higher levels of uncompensated care and rightfully demand that the reductions in Medicare payments be restored. Without the insurance mandate, creative new legislation will be required to maintain balance within the ACA.

A potential substitute for the insurance mandate is a late enrollment penalty. Medicare has had an insurance mandate for Medicare Part D (the drug benefit) since 2005 which seems to have been readily accepted by Medicare beneficiaries. Here is how it works. When an individual is eligible for Medicare, he must enroll in Part D or pay a penalty. This penalty applies when he does obtain Part D coverage and includes additional payment of 1 percent of the average cost of coverage for those months he does not have Part D. However, if he continues to work and can demonstrate "creditable coverage" for drug coverage through his employer-based insurance, the penalty does not apply (CMS 2011).

For example, assume a participant was on Medicare for two years without a drug plan, and this year she wants to enroll. The penalty is 1 percent of the average of all drug plans per month, which amounts to around

30 cents. The penalty is permanent, which can add up, as two years' (or 24 months') worth of penalties can raise the premium by more than $7 a month, perpetually. Because the cheapest Part D plans run between $15 and $18 per month, most experts recommend that even if an individual is on few or no medications, she should enroll in the least expensive plan.

If the insurance mandate is found unconstitutional, it will likely be replaced with alternatives such as the Medicare Part D penalty.

Standard Benefits

Although a standard benefit set in the HIEs levels the playing field for health plan competition, it also creates other challenges. For example, providers of services not included in the standard benefit set will lobby for inclusion; if more services are included, the cost of insurance will increase.

Another problem with standard benefits is that they are standard. They prevent health plans from developing creative policies that are less expensive or customized for unique markets. The standard benefit regulations will be a battleground for special interests; this might force changes in the ACA.

Medicaid Funding Requirement of States

The ACA provides 100 percent funding for the increased state portion of Medicaid, but only from 2014 to 2016. After that time, federal support gradually declines. For states that have low income-eligibility levels before 2014, this change will be expensive over the long term. Although increased levels of income eligibility are a key way the ACA increases insurance coverage in the United States, state pressure may change this policy.

Taxes

The ACA contains many new taxes on individuals, health plans, device manufacturers, tanning salons, and more. The political makeup of Congress and the presidency will affect the level of interest in changing these revenue-raising policies. However, these taxes are important to funding the subsidies in the HIEs and Medicaid. If they are repealed, the funds will need to be replaced through other sources.

Comparative Effectiveness Research

Evidence-based medicine was once derided as "cookbook medicine." Although that attitude has changed significantly, some providers still resist—particularly those that provide care that may be of limited benefit. Although research funded by the ACA is not supposed to be used for payment policy, Medicare and Medicaid will not continue to pay for services not found to be effective. Providers and suppliers will realize the effect on their incomes, which may lead to an attack on this segment of the ACA.

Independent Payment Advisory Board

The addition of this board was resisted by providers during the legislative debate but finally included as a blunt tool to control healthcare inflation. If the many cost-saving policies in the ACA work well, it will not be needed. However, if they do not, this board will be given more flexibility to devise payment solutions beyond reducing fee-for-service rates.

A more flexible solution that is effective in controlling costs is to use global budgets for hospitals and caps for physician salaries. If this strategy sounds familiar, it is—look north to Canada.

Malpractice

The ACA contains state demonstration projects to reduce malpractice expense (§10607). During the debate surrounding the ACA, Republicans pushed for much stronger policies; these new policies may be enacted as part of a bargain to retain other segments of the law.

The Public Option

The concept of a government-run health plan (probably Medicare) as part of the HIEs was highly controversial during the legislative process and was dropped from the final bill. However, if healthcare inflation appears to be uncontrollable before the start of the HIEs in 2014 and if the Democrats retake the House in 2012, a public option might make a comeback.

GOOD IDEAS LIKELY TO REMAIN

Health Insurance Exchanges

Although many conservatives do not like the insurance mandate, they do support health plan competition as a markets solution to healthcare costs. The HIEs provide a useful and contemporary system to foster competition (as with travel websites or eBay, for example). However, the standard benefit feature might be modified to provide for a wider range of products, which would allow for different benefits, deductibles, and coinsurance. In addition, subsidy levels may be modified if the ACA funding sources (taxes) are reduced or eliminated. Massachusetts and Utah (Utah Health Exchange 2011) provide alternative working models of state insurance exchanges.

Quality, Workforce, Fraud, and Innovation

The goals of increasing quality, increasing the supply of primary care practitioners, and fighting fraud have never been controversial. However, funding for these activities might be reduced based on general federal budget concerns.

The Center for Medicare and Medicaid Innovation had broad support in the policy community but may be modified, as it has taken some authority away from Congress.

ACOs, Bundled Payments, Readmissions, and Hospital-Acquired Conditions

These financial incentives and penalties for ACOs, bundled payments, readmissions, and hospital-acquired conditions are built on years of research and demonstration projects and would probably have been enacted without the ACA. These initiatives will likely continue but be modified as results become available.

WHAT ABOUT A REPEAL?

If candidates who run for Congress and the presidency in 2012 run against the ACA and win, total repeal is a possibility. However, healthcare inflation may prevent this. If inflation is untamed, health insurance will become unaffordable for individuals, employers, and the government.

Minnesota presents an interesting example of the possibilities for reductions in healthcare inflation. Since about 2001, Minnesota providers and the state government have invested in many of the key features of the ACA, including integrated provider systems, HIT, and the use of comparative effective research through the Institute for Clinical Systems Improvement (ICSI 2011). In 2008, Minnesota spent 13.4 percent of its GDP on healthcare, while the rest of the country spent 15.1 percent (Minnesota Department of Health 2010). This meant that Minnesota could spend over $4 billion of its wealth on private sector job creation and other growth strategies rather than on healthcare.

States that allow their healthcare systems to inflate beyond the national rate of healthcare inflation will be at a disadvantage in national and global competition. Therefore substantial segments of the ACA likely will be preserved to support policies and programs to reduce healthcare inflation.

STRATEGY THEMES FOR THE FUTURE

The ACA is likely to be changed, modified, and improved. Other forces will also affect the US healthcare system. The scenario planning exercises throughout this book suggest themes to be considered in strategy development.

- *Chronic disease management*—The greatest costs in a system are for care for patients with chronic disease. Effective systems of care need to be implemented, and the ACA rewards this behavior.
- *Greater use of HIT*—Automation holds great promise to improve care delivery and reduce cost. Funding for these new systems is available from the ARRA.
- *Community and population health*—Providers need to transition strategies away from episodes of acute care to systems to improve the health of a community. The ACA encourages a population view of healthcare.
- *Financial incentives for quality and efficiency*—Payers are moving from payment for the quantity of service to payment for value. Public reporting of quality will increase and providers that deliver high-quality services will be rewarded.
- *Closer integration with all parts of the system, particularly physicians*—Integrated systems have been shown to deliver high-quality, low-cost care. The ACA supports and rewards systems-based care.
- *New relationships with health plans*—Health insurance exchanges and accountable care organizations allow providers and health plans to work together in innovative care delivery systems.

HOW TO DO HEALTH POLICY

This is an invitation for you, the reader, to get into the game. Active participation, innovation, and creativity built the US government, and your expertise is needed. The thoughtful healthcare leader has three opportunities to become involved: through associations, through innovations and demonstrations, and as a policy expert.

Healthcare Associations and Lobbying

The easiest path for involvement in health policy is through the numerous healthcare associations. They may represent organizations (e.g., American Hospital Association) or individual professionals (e.g., American Medical Association). Much of the US healthcare system is affected by governmental policy; most associations have a legislative affairs committee. By joining these committees, leaders have an opportunity to shape and influence policy. Start with state associations, as these are more accessible and much of the ACA will be implemented through state legislation and regulation.

Within these committees, members can fill two roles. One role is to create policy positions (e.g., "we need to increase the supply of nurse practitioners") and the other is to direct advocacy—otherwise known as lobbying.

Because of the intensity of the arena, lobbying is not for the faint of heart or those with thin skins. However, it can be deeply rewarding and can have a significant and wide-reaching effect on your community.

Healthcare professionals who want to be become effective lobbyists should

- Develop a 30-second "elevator speech" about your proposal. Successful pitches can lead to appointments with elected officials for more in-depth briefings. Here is an example:

  Hello Senator Berglin, I am Dan McLaughlin, the CEO of Vincent Valley Health System, and we have an interesting proposal for our state that could reduce obesity in children by 25 percent through a cooperative program with schools and hospitals. Can I come to your office and provide you with more details?

- Know the topic. Once you have your meeting scheduled, be able to present your proposal in depth or briefly. Know who knows the topic in more depth so you can refer the official's staff to them if they want to explore the topic further.

- Know the legislative process. Never ask a legislator to do something that is prohibited by the rules (e.g., introduce a bill into the wrong committee). Engage a professional lobbyist to provide you with this information.
- Know the opposition. Surprisingly, the most innocent policy proposal will have opposition (in some cases bureaucrats protecting budgets or turf). Your elected official may agree to carry your legislative proposal; your duty is to provide her with information on the opposition and its arguments.
- Be respectful. Almost all elected officials strive to do the best for their constituencies and the country. They are almost never thanked and frequently take abuse from the general public. A thank you for their service will be highly appreciated.

Innovations in Care Delivery

The Center for Medicare and Medicaid Innovation is designed to experiment with new delivery and payment systems. If your organization has developed an innovation, consider applying to CMI to execute a pilot. If your innovation is a success it may be the basis for ACA version 2.

Policy Expertise

The third option to influence policy is to become an expert for an elected official. Most legislators choose one of two paths while in office. The first path is to focus on leadership, which requires an emphasis on party relationships, fundraising, media appearances, and the like. The second path is to focus on policy and become an expert in some subject. These legislators tend to craft the details of legislation and rely on experts to assist them. You can be their expert.

One of the most famous examples of this approach was chronicled in the book *The Dance of Legislation* by Eric Redman (2001). In 1971, Dr. Abe Berman of Seattle became passionate about physician shortages in underserved areas of the country. He met regularly with Senator Warren Magnuson and his staff to press the issue. Eventually Magnuson authored legislation to address this problem and did what was necessary to get it passed and signed by President

Nixon. The legislation continues today as the National Health Service Corps, which is expanded in the ACA, Title V.

SUMMARY

All laws are modified by future legislatures, and the ACA will be as well. Policies in the law that have high probability of change include the insurance mandate, standard benefits, funding for expanded Medicaid, taxes, comparative effectiveness research, the Independent Payment Advisory Board, and malpractice reform. If healthcare inflation continues unabated, the public option might again receive serious consideration.

Key policies in the ACA unlikely to be significantly changed include health insurance exchanges; quality improvement and reporting; workforce enhancements; financial incentives and penalties for accountable care organizations, bundled payments, readmissions, and hospital-acquired conditions; and the Center for Medicare and Medicaid Innovation.

Because the ACA creates a new environment for providers, a number of strategic themes need consideration: chronic disease management, the use of HIT, community and population health, financial incentives for quality and efficiency, integration of the system, and relationships between providers and health plans.

Healthcare leaders can participate in the policy process through healthcare associations and pilot programs sponsored by the government and by offering their expertise to elected officials.

CONCLUSION

The Affordable Care Act of 2010 is a remarkable legislative achievement. However, it will only serve the country well if healthcare leaders make the many needed changes supported by the law. Energetic healthcare leadership can ensure that the US healthcare system will lead the world in quality and effectiveness for many years.

ANNOTATED REFERENCES

CMS. 2011. "Creditable Coverage and Late Enrollment Penalty." [Online information; retrieved 1/24/11.] www.cms.gov/MedicarePresDrugEligEnrol/02_CreditableCoverageLateEnrollmentPenalty.asp

Institute for Clinical Systems Improvement (ICSI). 2011. [Online information; retrieved 1/14/11.] www.icsi.org/index.aspx?catID=2

The Institute for Clinical Systems Improvement (ICSI) was founded in 1993 by HealthPartners Medical Group, the Mayo Clinic, and Park Nicollet Health Services. ICSI today is the Upper Midwest's leading healthcare collaborative. It is funded by six Minnesota and Wisconsin health plans and is composed of 55 dues-paying medical groups and hospitals representing more than 9,000 physicians.

As an independent, nonprofit organization, ICSI helps its members implement best clinical practices for their patients. ICSI also works to transform the healthcare system so members and sponsors can deliver higher-quality and more affordable care. Its trusted collaborative processes have demonstrated ICSI's ability to bring diverse stakeholders together to champion system-based improvements in healthcare.

Minnesota Department of Health. 2010. *Minnesota Health Care Spending and Projections,* 3. St. Paul, MN: Minnesota Department of Health.

Redman, E. 2001. *The Dance of Legislation.* Seattle: University of Washington Press.

Utah Health Exchange. 2011. [Online information; retrieved 1/24/11.] www.exchange.utah.gov/

Discussion Questions

THE FOLLOWING QUESTIONS can be used by healthcare leaders with their teams to formulate strategy to succeed in the reformed environment. The Kaiser Foundation summary can be downloaded and read first by all team members (www.kff.org/healthreform/upload/8061.pdf); some may wish to read sections of the ACA itself. These questions can also be used to develop possible future scenarios (see the Introduction) to test the robustness of strategic plans.

1. EXPANDED COVERAGE

In 2014 the ACA will insure 30 million more Americans. What effect will this new large group of consumers/patients have on the delivery system? What can be done now to anticipate these new consumers?

2. HEALTH INSURANCE EXCHANGES

Also in 2014 individuals and employees at small employers will purchase their health insurance through state-based health insurance exchanges. What will be the effect of these new exchanges on health plans? On providers?

3. CHRONIC DISEASE MANAGEMENT

Patients with five or more chronic conditions account for 66 percent of the costs of Medicare. The ACA provides a number of policies to improve chronic disease management. What specific steps can providers (your organization) take to improve in chronic disease management? What are the barriers to improvement?

4. PRIMARY CARE

The ACA contains a number of policies to encourage the growth of primary care including new funds for workforce development and the healthcare home. In the face of much higher salaries paid to specialty physicians, can this strategy succeed? Are there other steps that should be taken today to improve the delivery of primary care?

5. QUALITY: REPORTING AND VALUE PURCHASING

Improved quality reporting and new pay-for-performance systems are part of the ACA. Will these systems be able to overcome the financial incentives in the system to provide care that is of questionable benefit to the patient?

6. PREVENTION AND WELLNESS

The ACA provides first-dollar coverage for many preventive services. It also allows employers to refund up to 30 percent of the cost of health insurance to employees if they participate and succeed in wellness programs. Will these efforts reduce the need for acute care services?

7. FINANCING: MEDICARE RATE INCREASES

To fund subsidies for low-income consumers' health insurance, the ACA reduces future Medicare payments to providers. Can providers reduce their costs sufficiently in this environment to remain financially healthy?

8. MANAGING RISK: ACOS AND BUNDLED PAYMENTS

The ACA provides an opportunity for providers to gain financially by accepting risk for population health (through accountable care organizations) or an episode of care (bundled payments). What organization form and tools are needed for providers to succeed with these new payment systems?

9. IMPACT ON THE SAFETY NET

Many of the uninsured and underinsured have been cared for by safety-net providers (i.e., public hospitals, community clinics, rural providers). With the substantial increase in insurance rates because of the ACA, what future role should safety-net providers fulfill?

10. WHAT NEEDS TO BE CHANGED?

"Health care reform is a journey, not a destination" (Senator Dave Durenberger). Since state and federal laws are amended each year, the ACA will change. What are priorities for change? What should be left alone?

Congressional Research Service
Summary of the ACA

The Affordable Care Act (ACA)

Healthcare reform legislation was introduced in September 2009, passed by the Senate in December, and passed by the House in March 2010. On March 23, 2010, the Patient Protection and Affordable Care Act was made into law (H.R.3590). After both chambers of Congress approved the original bill, another law was enacted to improve certain aspects of the original. This bill, the Health Care & Education Reconciliation Act (H.R.4872), was passed under the reconciliation process, which is why it contains a section on funding higher education. The Affordable Care Act is the combination of the two bills. Following are summaries of both the Patient Protection and Affordable Care Act and the Health Care & Education Reconciliation Act. These summaries were produced by the Congressional Research Service of the Library of Congress.

The Patient Protection and
Affordable Care Act (H.R.3590)

Sponsor: Rep Charles B. Rangel [NY-15] (introduced 9/17/2009)   Cosponsors (40)
Became Public Law No: 111-148

Title I: Quality, Affordable Health Care for All Americans

Subtitle A: Immediate Improvements in Health Care Coverage for All Americans

(Sec. 1001, as modified by Sec. 10101) Amends the Public Health Service Act to prohibit a health plan ("health plan" under this subtitle excludes any "grandfathered health plan" as defined in section 1251) from establishing lifetime limits or annual limits on the dollar value of benefits for any participant or beneficiary after January 1, 2014. Permits a restricted annual limit for plan years beginning prior to January 1, 2014. Declares that a health plan shall not be prevented from placing annual or lifetime per-beneficiary limits on covered benefits that are not essential health benefits to the extent that such limits are otherwise permitted.

Prohibits a health plan from rescinding coverage of an enrollee except in the case of fraud or intentional misrepresentation of material fact.

Requires health plans to provide coverage for, and to not impose any cost sharing requirements for: (1) specified preventive items or services; (2) recommended immunizations; and (3) recommended preventive care and screenings for women and children.

Requires a health plan that provides dependent coverage of children to make such coverage available for an unmarried, adult child until the child turns 26 years of age.

Requires the Secretary of Health and Human Services (HHS) to develop standards for health plans (including grandfathered health plans) to provide an accurate summary of benefits and coverage explanation. Directs each such health plan, prior to any enrollment restriction, to provide such a summary of benefits and coverage explanation to: (1) the applicant at the time of application; (2) an enrollee prior to the time of enrollment or re-enrollment; and (3) a policy or certificate holder at the time of issuance of the policy or delivery of the certificate.

Requires group health plans to comply with requirements relating to the prohibition against discrimination in favor of highly compensated individuals.

Requires the Secretary to develop reporting requirements for health plans on benefits or reimbursement structures that: (1) improve health outcomes; (2) prevent hospital readmissions; (3) improve patient safety and reduce medical errors; and (4) promote wellness and health.

Requires a health plan (including a grandfathered health plan) to: (1) submit to the Secretary a report concerning the ratio of the incurred loss (or incurred claims) plus the loss adjustment expense (or change in contract reserves) to earned premiums; and (2) provide an annual rebate to each enrollee if the ratio of the amount of premium revenue expended by the issuer on reimbursement for clinical services provided to enrollees and activities that improve health care quality to the total amount of premium revenue for the plan year is less than 85% for large group markets or 80% for small group or individual markets.

Requires each U.S. hospital to establish and make public a list of its standard charges for items and services.

Requires a health plan to implement an effective process for appeals of coverage determinations and claims.

Sets forth requirements for health plans related to: (1) designation of a primary care provider; (2) coverage of emergency services; and (3) elimination of referral requirements for obstetrical or gynecological care.

(Sec. 1002) Requires the Secretary to award grants to states for offices of health insurance consumer assistance or health insurance ombudsman programs.

(Sec. 1003, as modified by Sec. 10101) Requires the Secretary to establish a process for the annual review of unreasonable increases in premiums for health insurance coverage.

(Sec. 1004) Makes this subtitle effective for plan years beginning six months after enactment of this Act, with certain exceptions.

Subtitle B: Immediate Actions to Preserve and Expand Coverage

(Sec. 1101) Requires the Secretary to establish a temporary high risk health insurance pool program to provide health insurance coverage to eligible individuals with a preexisting condition. Terminates such coverage on January 1, 2014, and provides for a transition to an American Health Benefit Exchange (Exchange).

(Sec. 1102, as modified by Sec. 10102) Requires the Secretary to establish a temporary reinsurance program to provide reimbursement to participating employment-based plans for a portion of the cost of providing health insurance coverage to early retirees before January 1, 2014.

(Sec. 1103, as modified by Sec. 10102) Requires the Secretary to establish a mechanism, including an Internet website, through which a resident of, or small business in, any state may identify affordable health insurance coverage options in that state.

(Sec. 1104) Sets forth provisions governing electronic health care transactions. Establishes penalties for health plans failing to comply with requirements.

(Sec. 1105) Makes this subtitle effective on the date of enactment of this Act.

Subtitle C: Quality Health Insurance Coverage for All Americans

Part I: Health Insurance Market Reforms

(Sec. 1201, as modified by Sec. 10103) Prohibits a health plan ("health plan" under this subtitle excludes any "grandfathered health plan" as defined in section 1251) from: (1) imposing any preexisting condition exclusion; or (2) discriminating on the basis of any health status-related factor. Allows premium rates to vary only by individual or family coverage, rating area, age, or tobacco use.

Requires health plans in a state to: (1) accept every employer and individual in the state that applies for coverage; and (2) renew or continue coverage at the option of the plan sponsor or the individual, as applicable.

Prohibits a health plan from establishing individual eligibility rules based on health status-related factors, including medical condition, claims experience, receipt of health care, medical history, genetic information, and evidence of insurability.

Sets forth provisions governing wellness programs under the health plan, including allowing cost variances for coverage for participation in such a program.

Prohibits a health plan from discriminating with respect to participation under the plan or coverage against any health care provider who is acting within the scope of that provider's license or certification under applicable state law.

Requires health plans that offer health insurance coverage in the individual or small group market to ensure that such coverage includes the essential health benefits package. Requires a group health plan to ensure that any annual cost-sharing imposed under the plan does not exceed specified limitations.

Prohibits a health plan from: (1) applying any waiting period for coverage that exceeds 90 days; or (2) discriminating against individual participation in clinical trials with respect to treatment of cancer or any other life-threatening disease or condition.

Part II: Other Provisions

(Sec. 1251, as modified by Sec. 10103) Provides that nothing in this Act shall be construed to require that an individual terminate coverage under a group health plan or health insurance coverage in which such individual was enrolled on the date of enactment of this Act. Allows family members of individuals currently enrolled in a plan to enroll in such plan or coverage if such enrollment was permitted under the terms of the plan. Allows new employees and their families to enroll in a group health plan that provides coverage on the date of enactment of this Act.

Defines a "grandfathered health plan" as a group health plan or health insurance coverage in which an individual was enrolled on the date of enactment of this Act.

States that this subtitle and subtitle A shall not apply to: (1) a group health plan or health insurance coverage in which an individual was enrolled on the date of enactment of this Act, regardless of whether the individual renews such coverage after such date of enactment; (2) an existing group health plan that enrolls new employees under this section; and (3) health insurance coverage maintained pursuant to one or more collective bargaining agreements between employee representatives and one or more employers that was ratified before the date of enactment of this Act until the date on which the last of the collective bargaining agreements relating to the coverage terminates.

Applies provisions related to uniform coverage documents and medical loss ratios to grandfathered health plans for plan years beginning after enactment of this Act.

(Sec. 1252) Requires uniform application of standards or requirements adopted by states to all health plans in each applicable insurance market.

(Sec. 1253, as added by Sec. 10103) Directs the Secretary of Labor to prepare an annual report on self-insured group health plans and self-insured employers.

(Sec. 1254, as added by Sec. 10103) Requires the HHS Secretary to conduct a study of the fully-insured and self-insured group health plan markets related to financial solvency and the effect of insurance market reforms.

(Sec. 1255, as modified by Sec. 10103) Sets forth effective dates for specified provisions of this subtitle.

Subtitle D: Available Coverage Choices for All Americans

Part I: Establishment of Qualified Health Plans

(Sec. 1301, as modified by Sec. 10104) Defines "qualified health plan" to require that such a plan provides essential health benefits and offers at least one plan in the silver level and one plan in the gold level in each Exchange through which such plan is offered.

(Sec. 1302, as modified by Sec. 10104) Requires the essential health benefits package to provide essential health benefits and limit cost-sharing. Directs the Secretary to: (1) define essential health benefits and include emergency services, hospitalization, maternity and newborn care, mental health and substance use disorder services, prescription drugs, preventive and wellness services and chronic disease management, and pediatric services, including oral and vision care; (2) ensure that the scope of the essential health benefits is equal to the scope of benefits provided under a typical employer plan; and (3) provide notice and an opportunity for public comment in defining the essential health benefits. Establishes: (1) an annual limit on cost-sharing beginning in 2014; and (2) a limitation on the deductible under a small group market health plan.

Sets forth levels of coverage for health plans defined by a certain percentage of the costs paid by the plan. Allows health plans in the individual market to offer catastrophic coverage for individuals under age 30, with certain limitations.

(Sec. 1303, as modified by Sec. 10104) Sets forth special rules for abortion coverage, including: (1) permitting states to elect to prohibit abortion coverage in qualified health plans offered through an Exchange in the state; (2) prohibiting federal funds from being used for abortion services; and (3) requiring separate accounts for payments for such services. Prohibits any qualified health plan offered through an Exchange from discriminating against any individual health care provider or health care facility because of its unwillingness to provide, pay for, provide coverage of, or refer for abortions.

(Sec. 1304, as modified by Sec. 10104) Sets forth definitions for terms used in this title.

Part II: Consumer Choices and Insurance Competition Through Health Benefit Exchanges

(Sec. 1311, as modified by Sec. 10104) Requires states to establish an American Health Benefit Exchange that: (1) facilitates the purchase of qualified health plans; and (2) provides for the establishment of a Small Business Health Options Program (SHOP Exchange) that is designed to assist qualified small employers in facilitating the enrollment of their employees in qualified health plans offered in the small group market in the state.

Requires the Secretary to establish criteria for the certification of health plans as qualified health plans, including requirements for: (1) meeting market requirements; and (2) ensuring a sufficient choice of providers.

Sets forth the requirements for an Exchange, including that an Exchange: (1) must be a governmental agency or nonprofit entity that is established by a state; (2) may not make available any health plan that is not a qualified health plan; (3) must implement procedures for certification of health plans as qualified health plans; and (4) must require health plans seeking certification to submit a justification of any premium increase prior to implementation of such increase.

Permits states to require qualified health plans to offer additional benefits. Requires states to pay for the cost of such additional benefits.

Allows a state to establish one or more subsidiary Exchanges for geographically distinct areas of a certain size.

Applies mental health parity provisions to qualified health plans.

(Sec. 1312, as modified by Sec. 10104) Allows an employer to select a level of coverage to be made available to employees through an Exchange. Allows employees to choose to enroll in any qualified health plan that offers that level of coverage.

Restricts the health plans that the federal government may make available to Members of Congress and congressional staff after the effective date of this subtitle to only those health plans that are created under this Act or offered through an Exchange.

Permits states to allow large employers to join an Exchange after 2017.

(Sec. 1313, as modified by Sec. 10104) Requires an Exchange to keep an accurate accounting of all activities, receipts, and expenditures and to submit to the Secretary, annually, a report concerning such accountings. Requires the Secretary to take certain action to reduce fraud and abuse in the administration of this title. Requires the Comptroller General to conduct an ongoing study of Exchange activities and the enrollees in qualified health plans offered through Exchanges.

Part III: State Flexibility Relating to Exchanges

(Sec. 1321) Requires the Secretary to issue regulations setting standards related to: (1) the establishment and operation of Exchanges; (2) the offering of qualified health plans through Exchanges; and (3) the establishment of the reinsurance and risk adjustment programs under part V.

Requires the Secretary to: (1) establish and operate an Exchange within a state if the state does not have one operational by January 1, 2014; and (2) presume that an Exchange operating in a state before January 1, 2010, that insures a specified percentage of its population meets the standards under this section.

(Sec. 1322, as modified by Sec. 10104) Requires the Secretary to establish the Consumer Operated and Oriented Plan (CO-OP) program to foster the creation of qualified nonprofit health insurance issuers to offer qualified health plans in the individual and small group markets. Requires the Secretary to provide for loans and grants to persons applying to become qualified nonprofit health insurance issuers. Sets forth provisions governing the establishment and operation of CO-OP program plans.

(Sec. 1323, deleted by Sec. 10104)

(Sec. 1324, as modified by Sec. 10104) Declares that health insurance coverage offered by a private health insurance issuer shall not be subject to federal or state laws if a qualified health plan offered under the CO-OP program is not subject to such law.

Part IV: State Flexibility to Establish Alternative Programs

(Sec. 1331, as modified by Sec. 10104) Requires the Secretary to establish a basic health program under which a state may enter into contracts to offer one or more standard health plans providing at least the essential health benefits to eligible individuals in lieu of offering such individuals coverage through an Exchange. Sets forth requirements for such a plan. Transfers funds that would have gone to the Exchange for such individuals to the state.

(Sec. 1332) Authorizes a state to apply to the Secretary for the waiver of specified requirements under this Act with respect to health insurance coverage within that state for plan years beginning on or after January 1, 2017. Directs the Secretary to provide for an alternative means by which the aggregate amounts of credits or reductions that would have been paid on behalf of participants in the Exchange will be paid to the state for purposes of implementing the state plan.

(Sec. 1333, as modified by Sec. 10104) Requires the Secretary to issue regulations for the creation of health care choice compacts under which two or more states may enter into an agreement that: (1) qualified health plans could be offered in the individual markets in all such states only subject to the laws and regulations of the state in which the plan was written or issued; and (2) the issuer of any qualified health plan to which the compact applies would continue to be subject to certain laws of the state in which the purchaser resides, would be required to be licensed in each state, and must clearly notify consumers that the policy may not be subject to all the laws and regulations of the state in which the purchaser resides. Sets forth provisions regarding the Secretary's approval of such compacts.

(Sec. 1334, as added by Sec. 10104) Requires the Director of the Office of Personnel Management (OPM) to: (1) enter into contracts with health insurance issuers to offer at least two multistate qualified health plans through each Exchange in each state to provide individual or group coverage; and (2) implement this subsection in a manner similar to the manner in which the Director implements the Federal Employees Health Benefits Program. Sets forth requirements for a multistate qualified health plan.

Part V: Reinsurance and Risk Adjustment

(Sec. 1341, as modified by Sec. 10104) Directs each state, not later than January 1, 2014, to establish one or more reinsurance entities to carry out the reinsurance program under this section. Requires the Secretary to establish standards to enable states to establish and maintain a reinsurance program under which: (1) health insurance issuers and third party administrators on behalf of group health plans are required to make payments to an applicable reinsurance entity for specified plan years; and (2) the applicable reinsurance entity uses amounts collected to make reinsurance payments to health insurance issuers that cover high-risk individuals in the individual market. Directs the state to eliminate or modify any state high-risk pool to the extent necessary to carry out the reinsurance program established under this section.

(Sec. 1342) Requires the Secretary to establish and administer a program of risk corridors for calendar years 2014 through 2016 under which a qualified health plan offered in the individual or small group market shall participate in a payment-adjusted system based on the ratio of the allowable costs of the plan to the plan's aggregate premiums. Directs the Secretary to make payments when a plan's allowable costs exceed the target amount by a certain percentage and directs a plan to make payments to the Secretary when its allowable costs are less than target amount by a certain percentage.

(Sec. 1343) Requires each state to assess a charge on health plans and health insurance issuers if the actuarial risk of the enrollees of such plans or coverage for a year is less than the average actuarial risk of all enrollees in all plans or coverage in the state for the year. Requires each state to provide a payment to health plans and health insurance issuers if the actuarial risk of the enrollees of such plan or coverage for a year is greater than the average actuarial risk of all enrollees in all plans and coverage in the state for the year. Excludes self-insured group health plans from this section.

Subtitle E: Affordable Coverage Choices for All Americans

Part I: Premium Tax Credits and Cost-sharing Reductions

Subpart A: Premium Tax Credits and Cost-sharing Reductions   (Sec. 1401, as modified by section 10105) Amends the Internal Revenue Code to allow individual taxpayers whose household income equals or exceeds 100%, but does not exceed 400%, of the federal poverty line (as determined in the Social Security Act [SSA]) a refundable tax credit for a percentage of the cost of premiums for coverage under a qualified health plan. Sets forth formulae and rules for the calculation of credit amounts based upon taxpayer household income as a percentage of the poverty line.

Directs the Comptroller General, not later than five years after enactment of this Act, to conduct a study and report to specified congressional committees on the affordability of health insurance coverage.

(Sec. 1402) Requires reductions in the maximum limits for out-of-pocket expenses for individuals enrolled in qualified health plans whose incomes are between 100% and 400% of the poverty line.

Subpart B: Eligibility Determinations (Sec. 1411)—Requires the Secretary to establish a program for verifying the eligibility of applicants for participation in a qualified health plan offered through an Exchange or for a tax credit for premium assistance based upon their income or their citizenship or immigration status. Requires an Exchange to submit information received from an applicant to the Secretary for verification of applicant eligibility. Provides for confidentiality of applicant information and for an appeals and redetermination process for denials of eligibility. Imposes civil penalties on applicants for providing false or fraudulent information relating to eligibility.

Requires the Secretary to study and report to Congress by January 1, 2013, on procedures necessary to ensure the protection of privacy and due process rights in making eligibility and other determinations under this Act.

(Sec. 1412) Requires the Secretary to establish a program for advance payments of the tax credit for premium assistance and for reductions of cost-sharing. Prohibits any federal payments, tax credit, or cost-sharing reductions for individuals who are not lawfully present in the United States.

(Sec. 1413) Requires the Secretary to establish a system to enroll state residents who apply to an Exchange in state health subsidy programs, including Medicaid or the Children's Health Insurance Program (CHIP, formerly known as SCHIP), if such residents are found to be eligible for such programs after screening.

(Sec. 1414) Requires the Secretary of the Treasury to disclose to HHS personnel certain taxpayer information to determine eligibility for programs under this Act or certain other social security programs.

(Sec. 1415) Disregards the premium assistance tax credit and cost-sharing reductions in determining eligibility for federal and federally-assisted programs.

(Sec. 1416, as added by section 10105) Directs the HHS Secretary to study and report to Congress by January 1, 2013, on the feasibility and implication of adjusting the application of the federal poverty level under this subtitle for different geographic areas in the United States, including its territories.

Part II: Small Business Tax Credit

(Sec. 1421, as modified by section 10105) Allows qualified small employers to elect, beginning in 2010, a tax credit for 50% of their employee health care coverage expenses. Defines "qualified small employer" as an employer who has no more than 25 employees with average annual compensation levels not exceeding $50,000. Requires a phase-out of such credit based on employer size and employee compensation.

Subtitle F: Shared Responsibility for Health Care

Part I: Individual Responsibility

(Sec. 1501, as modified by section 10106) Requires individuals to maintain minimal essential health care coverage beginning in 2014. Imposes a penalty for failure to maintain such coverage beginning in 2014, except for certain low-income individuals who cannot afford coverage, members of Indian tribes, and individuals who suffer hardship. Exempts from the coverage requirement individuals who object to health care coverage on religious grounds, individuals not lawfully present in the United States, and individuals who are incarcerated.

(Sec. 1502) Requires providers of minimum essential coverage to file informational returns providing identifying information of covered individuals and the dates of coverage. Requires the IRS to send a notice to taxpayers who are not enrolled in minimum essential coverage about services available through the Exchange operating in their state.

Part II: Employer Responsibilities

(Sec. 1511) Amends the Fair Labor Standards Act of 1938 to: (1) require employers with more than 200 full-time employees to automatically enroll new employees in a health care plan and provide notice of the opportunity to opt-out of such coverage; and (2) provide notice to employees about an Exchange, the availability of a tax credit for premium assistance, and the loss of an employer's contribution to an employer-provided health benefit plan if the employee purchases a plan through an Exchange.

(Sec. 1513, as modified by section 10106) Imposes fines on large employers (employers with more than 50 full-time employees) who fail to offer their full-time employees the opportunity to enroll in minimum essential coverage or who have a waiting period for enrollment of more than 60 days.

Requires the Secretary of Labor to study and report to Congress on whether employees' wages are reduced due to fines imposed on employers.

(Sec. 1514, as modified by section 10106) Requires large employers to file a report with the Secretary of the Treasury on health insurance coverage provided to their full-time employees. Requires such reports to contain: (1) a certification as to whether such employers provide their full-time employees (and their dependents) the opportunity to enroll in minimum essential coverage under an eligible employer-sponsored plan; (2) the length of any waiting period for such coverage; (3) the months during which such coverage was available; (4) the monthly premium for the lowest cost option in each of the enrollment categories under the plan; (5) the employer's share of the total allowed costs of benefits provided under the plan; and (6) identifying information about the employer and full-time employees. Imposes a penalty on employers who fail to provide such report. Authorizes the Secretary of the Treasury to review the accuracy of information provided by large employers.

(Sec. 1515) Allows certain small employers to include as a benefit in a tax-exempt cafeteria plan a qualified health plan offered through an Exchange.

Subtitle G: Miscellaneous Provisions

(Sec. 1551) Applies the definitions under the Public Health Service Act related to health insurance coverage to this title.

(Sec. 1552) Requires the HHS Secretary to publish on the HHS website a list of all of the authorities provided to the Secretary under this Act.

(Sec. 1553) Prohibits the federal government, any state or local government or health care provider that receives federal financial assistance under this Act, or any health plan created under this Act from discriminating against an individual or institutional health care entity on the basis that such individual or entity does not provide a health care item or service furnished for the purpose of causing, or assisting in causing, the death of any individual, such as by assisted suicide, euthanasia, or mercy killing.

(Sec. 1554) Prohibits the Secretary from promulgating any regulation that: (1) creates an unreasonable barrier to the ability of individuals to obtain appropriate medical care; (2) impedes timely access to health care services; (3) interferes with communications regarding a full range of treatment options between the patient and the health care provider; (4) restricts the ability of health care providers to provide full disclosure of all relevant information to patients making health care decisions; (5) violates the principle of informed consent and the ethical standards of health care professionals; or (6) limits the availability of health care treatment for the full duration of a patient's medical needs.

(Sec. 1555) Declares that no individual, company, business, nonprofit entity, or health insurance issuer offering group or individual health insurance coverage shall be required to participate in any federal health insurance program created by or expanded under this Act. Prohibits any penalty from being imposed upon any such issuer for choosing not to participate in any such program.

(Sec. 1556) Amends the Black Lung Benefits Act, with respect to claims filed on or after the effective date of the Black Lung Benefits Amendments of 1981, to eliminate exceptions to: (1) the applicability of certain provisions regarding rebuttable presumptions; and (2) the prohibition against requiring eligible survivors of a miner determined to be eligible for black lung benefits to file a new claim or to refile or otherwise revalidate the miner's claim.

(Sec. 1557) Prohibits discrimination by any federal health program or activity on the grounds of race, color, national origin, sex, age, or disability.

(Sec. 1558) Amends the Fair Labor Standards Act of 1938 to prohibit an employer from discharging or discriminating against any employee because the employee: (1) has received a health insurance credit or subsidy; (2) provides information relating to any violation of any provision of such Act; or (3) objects to, or refuses to participate in, any activity, policy, practice, or assigned task that the employee reasonably believed to be in violation of such Act.

(Sec. 1559) Gives the HHS Inspector General oversight authority with respect to the administration and implementation of this title.

(Sec. 1560) Declares that nothing in this title shall be construed to modify, impair, or supersede the operation of any antitrust laws.

(Sec. 1561) Amends the Public Health Service Act to require the Secretary to: (1) develop interoperable and secure standards and protocols that facilitate enrollment of individuals in federal and state health and human services programs; and (2) award grants to develop and adapt technology systems to implement such standards and protocols.

(Sec. 1562, as added by Sec. 10107) Directs the Comptroller General to study denials by health plans of coverage for medical services and of applications to enroll in health insurance.

(Sec. 1563, as added by Sec. 10107) Disallows the waiver of laws or regulations establishing procurement requirements relating to small business concerns with respect to any contract awarded under any program or other authority under this Act.

(Sec. 1563 [sic], as modified by Sec. 10107) Makes technical and conforming amendments.

(Sec. 1563 [sic]) Expresses the sense of the Senate that: (1) the additional surplus in the Social Security trust fund generated by this Act should be reserved for Social Security; and (2) the net savings generated by the CLASS program (established under Title VIII of this Act) should be reserved for such program.

Title II: Role of Public Programs

Subtitle A: Improved Access to Medicaid

(Sec. 2001, as modified by Sec. 10201) Amends title XIX (Medicaid) of the SSA to extend Medicaid coverage, beginning in calendar 2014, to individuals under age 65 who are not entitled to or enrolled in Medicare and have incomes at or below 133% of the federal poverty line. Grants a state the option to expand Medicaid eligibility to such individuals as early as April 1, 2010. Provides that, for between 2014 and 2016, the federal government will pay 100% of the cost of covering newly-eligible individuals.

Increases the federal medical assistance percentage (FMAP): (1) with respect to newly eligible individuals; and (2) between January 1, 2014, and December 31, 2016, for states meeting certain eligibility requirements.

Requires Medicaid benchmark benefits to include coverage of prescription drugs and mental health services.

Grants states the option to extend Medicaid coverage to individuals who have incomes that exceed 133% of the federal poverty line beginning January 1, 2014.

(Sec. 2002) Requires a state to use an individual's or household's modified gross income to determine income eligibility for Medicaid for non-elderly individuals, without applying any income or expense disregards or assets or resources test.

Exempts from this requirement: (1) individuals eligible for Medicaid through another program; (2) the elderly or Social Security Disability Insurance (SSDI) program beneficiaries; (3) the medically needy; (4) enrollees in a Medicare Savings Program; and (5) the disabled.

(Sec. 2003) Revises state authority to offer a premium assistance subsidy for qualified employer-sponsored coverage to children under age 19 to extend such a subsidy to all individuals, regardless of age.

Prohibits a state from requiring, as a condition of Medicaid eligibility, that an individual (or the individual's parent) apply for enrollment in qualified employer-sponsored coverage.

(Sec. 2004, as modified by Sec. 10201) Extends Medicaid coverage to former foster care children who are under 26 years of age.

(Sec. 2005, as modified by Sec. 10201) Revises requirements for Medicaid payments to territories, including an increase in the limits on payments for FY2011 and thereafter.

(Sec. 2006, as modified by Sec. 10201) Prescribes an adjustment to the FMAP determination for certain states recovering from a major disaster.

(Sec. 2007) Rescinds any unobligated amounts available to the Medicaid Improvement Fund for FY2014-FY2018.

Subtitle B: Enhanced Support for the Children's Health Insurance Program

(Sec. 2101, as modified by Sec. 10201) Amends SSA title XXI (State Children's Health Insurance Program) (CHIP, formerly known as SCHIP) to increase the FY2016-FY2019 enhanced FMAP for states, subject to a 100% cap.

Prohibits states from applying, before the end of FY2019, CHIP eligibility standards that are more restrictive than those under this Act.

Deems ineligible for CHIP any targeted low-income children who cannot enroll in CHIP because allotments are capped, but who are therefore eligible for tax credits in the Exchanges.

Requires the Secretary to: (1) review benefits offered for children, and related cost-sharing imposed, by qualified health plans offered through an Exchange; and (2) certify those plans whose benefits and cost-sharing are at least comparable to those provided under the particular state's CHIP plan.

Prohibits enrollment bonus payments for children enrolled in CHIP after FY2013.

Requires a state CHIP plan, beginning January 1, 2014, to use modified gross income and household income to determine CHIP eligibility.

Requires a state to treat as a targeted low-income child eligible for CHIP any child determined ineligible for Medicaid as a result of the elimination of an income disregard based on expense or type of income.

(Sec. 2102) Makes technical corrections to the Children's Health Insurance Program Reauthorization Act of 2009 (CHIPRA).

Subtitle C: Medicaid and CHIP Enrollment Simplification

(Sec. 2201) Amends SSA title XIX (Medicaid) to require enrollment application simplification and coordination with state health insurance Exchanges and CHIP via state-run websites.

(Sec. 2202) Permits hospitals to provide Medicaid services during a period of presumptive eligibility to members of all Medicaid eligibility categories.

Subtitle D: Improvements to Medicaid Services

(Sec. 2301) Requires Medicaid coverage of: (1) freestanding birth center services; and (2) concurrent care for children receiving hospice care.

(Sec. 2303) Gives states the option of extending Medicaid coverage to family planning services and supplies under a presumptive eligibility period for a categorically needy group of individuals.

Subtitle E: New Options for States to Provide Long-Term Services and Supports

(Sec. 2401) Authorizes states to offer home and community-based attendant services and supports to Medicaid beneficiaries with disabilities who would otherwise require care in a hospital, nursing facility, intermediate care facility for the mentally retarded, or an institution for mental diseases.

(Sec. 2402) Gives states the option of: (1) providing home and community-based services to individuals eligible for services under a waiver; and (2) offering home and community-based services to specific, targeted populations.

Creates an optional eligibility category to provide full Medicaid benefits to individuals receiving home and community-based services under a state plan amendment.

(Sec. 2403) Amends the Deficit Reduction Act of 2005 to: (1) extend through FY2016 the Money Follows the Person Rebalancing Demonstration; and (2) reduce to 90 days the institutional residency period.

(Sec. 2404) Applies Medicaid eligibility criteria to recipients of home and community-based services, during calendar 2014 through 2019, in such a way as to protect against spousal impoverishment.

(Sec. 2405) Makes appropriations for FY2010-FY2014 to the Secretary, acting through the Assistant Secretary for Aging, to expand state aging and disability resource centers.

(Sec. 2406) Expresses the sense of the Senate that: (1) during the 111th session of Congress, Congress should address long-term services and supports in a comprehensive way that guarantees elderly and disabled individuals the care they need; and (2) long-term services and supports should be made available in the community in addition to institutions.

Subtitle F: Medicaid Prescription Drug Coverage

(Sec. 2501) Amends SSA title XIX (Medicaid) to: (1) increase the minimum rebate percentage for single source drugs and innovator multiple source drugs; (2) increase the rebate for other drugs; (3) require contracts with Medicaid managed care organizations to extend prescription drug rebates (discounts) to their enrollees; (4) provide an additional rebate for new formulations of existing drugs; and (5) set a maximum rebate amount.

(Sec. 2502) Eliminates the exclusion from Medicaid coverage of, thereby extending coverage to, certain drugs used to promote smoking cessation, as well as barbiturates and benzodiazepines.

(Sec. 2503) Revises requirements with respect to pharmacy reimbursements.

Subtitle G: Medicaid Disproportionate Share Hospital (DSH) Payments

(Sec. 2551, as modified by Sec. 10201) Reduces state disproportionate share hospital (DSH) allotments, except for Hawaii, by 50% or 35% once a state's uninsurance rate decreases by 45%, depending on whether they have spent at least or more than 99.9% of their allotments on average during FY2004-FY2008. Requires a reduction of only 25% or 17.5% for low DSH states, depending on whether they have spent at least or more than 99.9% of their allotments on average during FY2004-FY2008. Prescribes allotment reduction requirements for subsequent fiscal years.

Revises DSH allotments for Hawaii for the last three quarters of FY2012 and for FY2013 and succeeding fiscal years.

Subtitle H: Improved Coordination for Dual Eligible Beneficiaries

(Sec. 2601) Declares that any Medicaid waiver for individuals dually eligible for both Medicaid and Medicare may be conducted for a period of five years, with a five-year extension, upon state request, unless the Secretary determines otherwise for specified reasons.

(Sec. 2602) Directs the Secretary to establish a Federal Coordinated Health Care Office to bring together officers and employees of the Medicare and Medicaid programs at the Centers for Medicare and Medicaid Services (CMS) to: (1) integrate Medicaid and Medicare benefits more effectively; and (2) improve the coordination between the federal government and states for dual eligible individuals to ensure that they get full access to the items and services to which they are entitled.

Subtitle I: Improving the Quality of Medicaid for Patients and Providers

(Sec. 2701) Amends SSA title XI, as modified by CHIPRA, to direct the Secretary to: (1) identify and publish a recommended core set of adult health quality measures for Medicaid eligible adults; and (2) establish a Medicaid Quality Measurement Program.

(Sec. 2702) Requires the Secretary to identify current state practices that prohibit payment for health care-acquired conditions and to incorporate them, or elements of them, which are appropriate for application in regulations to the Medicaid program. Requires such regulations to prohibit payments to states for any amounts expended for providing medical assistance for specified health care-acquired conditions.

(Sec. 2703) Gives states the option to provide coordinated care through a health home for individuals with chronic conditions. Authorizes the Secretary to award planning grants to states to develop a state plan amendment to that effect.

(Sec. 2704) Directs the Secretary to establish a demonstration project to evaluate the use of bundled payments for the provision of integrated care for a Medicaid beneficiary: (1) with respect to an episode of care that includes a hospitalization; and (2) for concurrent physician services provided during a hospitalization.

(Sec. 2705) Requires the Secretary to establish a Medicaid Global Payment System Demonstration Project under which a participating state shall adjust payments made to an eligible safety net hospital or network from a fee-for-service payment structure to a global capitated payment model. Authorizes appropriations.

(Sec. 2706) Directs the Secretary to establish the Pediatric Accountable Care Organization Demonstration Project to authorize a participating state to allow pediatric medical providers meeting specified requirements to be recognized as an accountable care organization for the purpose of receiving specified incentive payments. Authorizes appropriations.

(Sec. 2707) Requires the Secretary to establish a three-year Medicaid emergency psychiatric demonstration project. Makes appropriations for FY2011.

Subtitle J: Improvements to the Medicaid and CHIP Payment and Access Commission (MACPAC)

(Sec. 2801) Revises requirements with respect to the Medicaid and CHIP Payment and Access Commission (MACPAC) and the Medicare Payment Advisory Commission (MEDPAC), including those for MACPAC membership, topics to be reviewed, and MEDPAC review of Medicaid trends in spending, utilization, and financial performance.

Requires MACPAC and MEDPAC to consult with one another on related issues.

Makes appropriations to MACPAC for FY2010.

Subtitle K: Protections for American Indians and Alaska Natives

(Sec. 2901) Sets forth special rules relating to Indians.

Declares that health programs operated by the Indian Health Service (IHS), Indian tribes, tribal organizations, and Urban Indian organizations shall be the payer of last resort for services they provide to eligible individuals.

Makes such organizations Express Lane agencies for determining Medicaid and CHIP eligibility.

(Sec. 2902) Makes permanent the requirement that the Secretary reimburse certain Indian hospitals and clinics for all Medicare Part B services.

Subtitle L: Maternal and Child Health Services

(Sec. 2951) Amends SSA title V (Maternal and Child Health Services) to direct the Secretary to make grants to eligible entities for early childhood home visitation programs. Makes appropriations for FY2010-FY2014.

(Sec. 2952) Encourages the Secretary to continue activities on postpartum depression or postpartum psychosis, including research to expand the understanding of their causes and treatment.

Authorizes the Secretary to make grants to eligible entities for projects to establish, operate, and coordinate effective and cost-efficient systems for the delivery of essential services to individuals with or at risk for postpartum conditions and their families. Authorizes appropriations for FY2010-FY2012.

(Sec. 2953, as modified by Sec. 10201) Directs the Secretary to allot funds to states to award grants to local organizations and other specified entities to carry out personal responsibility education programs to educate adolescents on both abstinence and contraception for the prevention of pregnancy and sexually transmitted infections, as well as on certain adulthood preparation subjects. Makes appropriations for FY2010-FY2014.

(Sec. 2954) Makes appropriations for FY2010-FY2014 for abstinence education.

(Sec. 2955) Requires the case review system for children aging out of foster care and independent living programs to include information about the importance of having a health care power of attorney in transition planning.

Title III: Improving the Quality and Efficiency of Health Care

Subtitle A: Transforming the Health Care Delivery System

Part I: Linking Payment to Quality Outcomes under the Medicare Program

(Sec. 3001) Amends SSA title XVIII (Medicare) to direct the Secretary to establish a hospital value-based purchasing program under which value-based incentive payments are made in a fiscal year to hospitals that meet specified performance standards for a certain performance period.

Directs the Secretary to establish value-based purchasing demonstration programs for: (1) inpatient critical access hospital services; and (2) hospitals excluded from the program because of insufficient numbers of measures and cases.

(Sec. 3002) Extends through 2013 the authority for incentive payments under the physician quality reporting system. Prescribes an incentive (penalty) for providers who do not report quality measures satisfactorily, beginning in 2015.

Requires the Secretary to integrate reporting on quality measures with reporting requirements for the meaningful use of electronic health records.

(Sec. 3003) Requires specified new types of reports and data analysis under the physician feedback program.

(Sec. 3004) Requires long-term care hospitals, inpatient rehabilitation hospitals, and hospices, starting in rate year 2014, to submit data on specified quality measures. Requires reduction of the annual update of entities which do not comply.

(Sec. 3005) Directs the Secretary, starting FY2014, to establish quality reporting programs for inpatient cancer hospitals exempt from the prospective payment system.

(Sec. 3006, as modified by Sec. 10301) Directs the Secretary to develop a plan to implement value-based purchasing programs for Medicare payments for skilled nursing facilities (SNFs), home health agencies, and ambulatory surgical centers.

(Sec. 3007) Directs the Secretary to establish a value-based payment modifier, under the physician fee schedule, based upon the quality of care furnished compared to cost.

(Sec. 3008) Subjects hospitals to a penalty adjustment to hospital payments for high rates of hospital acquired conditions.

Part II: National Strategy to Improve Health Care Quality

(Sec. 3011, as modified by Sec. 10302) Amends the Public Health Service Act to direct the Secretary, through a transparent collaborative process, to establish a National Strategy for Quality Improvement in health care services, patient health outcomes, and population health, taking into consideration certain limitations on the use of comparative effectiveness data.

(Sec. 3012) Directs the President to convene an Interagency Working Group on Health Care Quality.

(Sec. 3013, as modified by Sec. 10303) Directs the Secretary, at least triennially, to identify gaps where no quality measures exist as well as existing quality measures that need improvement, updating, or expansion, consistent with the national strategy for use in federal health programs.

Directs the Secretary to award grants, contracts, or intergovernmental agreements to eligible entities for purposes of developing, improving, updating, or expanding such quality measures.

Requires the Secretary to develop and update periodically provider-level outcome measures for hospitals and physicians, as well as other appropriate providers.

(Sec. 3014, as modified by Sec. 10304) Requires the convening of multi-stakeholder groups to provide input into the selection of quality and efficiency measures.

(Sec. 3015, as modified by Sec. 10305) Directs the Secretary to: (1) establish an overall strategic framework to carry out the public reporting of performance information; and (2) collect and aggregate consistent data on quality and resource use measures from information systems used to support health care delivery. Authorizes the Secretary to award grants for such purpose.

Directs the Secretary to make available to the public, through standardized Internet websites, performance information summarizing data on quality measures.

Part III: Encouraging Development of New Patient Care Models

(Sec. 3021, as modified by Sec. 10306) Creates within CMS a Center for Medicare and Medicaid Innovation to test innovative payment and service delivery models to reduce program expenditures while preserving or enhancing the quality of care furnished to individuals. Makes appropriations for FY2010-FY2019.

(Sec. 3022, as modified by Sec. 10307) Directs the Secretary to establish a shared savings program that: (1) promotes accountability for a patient population; (2) coordinates items and services under Medicare Parts A and B; and (3) encourages investment in infrastructure and redesigned care processes for high quality and efficient service delivery.

(Sec. 3023, as modified by Sec. 10308) Directs the Secretary to establish a pilot program for integrated care (involving payment bundling) during an episode of care provided to an applicable beneficiary around a hospitalization in order to improve the coordination, quality, and efficiency of health care services.

(Sec. 3024) Directs the Secretary to conduct a demonstration program to test a payment incentive and service delivery model that utilizes physician and nurse practitioner directed home-based primary care teams designed to reduce expenditures and improve health outcomes in the provision of items and services to applicable beneficiaries.

(Sec. 3025, as modified by Sec. 10309) Requires the Secretary to establish a hospital readmissions reduction program involving certain payment adjustments, effective for discharges on or after October 1, 2012, for certain potentially preventable Medicare inpatient hospital readmissions.

Directs the Secretary to make available a program for hospitals with a high severity adjusted readmission rate to improve their readmission rates through the use of patient safety organizations.

(Sec. 3026) Directs the Secretary to establish a Community-Based Care Transitions Program which provides funding to eligible entities that furnish improved care transitions services to high-risk Medicare beneficiaries.

(Sec. 3027) Amends the Deficit Reduction Act of 2005 to extend certain Gainsharing Demonstration Projects through FY2011.

Subtitle B: Improving Medicare for Patients and Providers

Part I: Ensuring Beneficiary Access to Physician Care and Other Services

(Sec. 3101, deleted by section 10310)

(Sec. 3102) Extends through calendar 2010 the floor on geographic indexing adjustments to the work portion of the physician fee schedule. Revises requirements for calculation of the practice expense portion of the geographic adjustment factor applied in a fee schedule area for services furnished in 2010 or 2011. Directs the Secretary to analyze current methods of establishing practice expense geographic adjustments and make appropriate further adjustments (a new methodology) to such adjustments for 2010 and subsequent years.

(Sec. 3103) Extends the process allowing exceptions to limitations on medically necessary therapy caps through December 31, 2010.

(Sec. 3104) Amends the Medicare, Medicaid, and SCHIP Benefits Improvement and Protection Act of 2000 to extend until January 1, 2010, an exception to a payment rule that permits laboratories to receive direct Medicare reimbursement when providing the technical component of certain physician pathology services that had been outsourced by certain (rural) hospitals.

(Sec. 3105, as modified by Sec. 10311) Amends SSA title XVIII (Medicare) to extend the bonus and increased payments for ground ambulance services until January 1, 2011.

Amends the Medicare Improvements for Patients and Providers Act of 2008 (MIPPA) to extend the payment of certain urban air ambulance services until January 1, 2011.

(Sec. 3106, as modified by Sec. 10312) Amends the Medicare, Medicaid, and SCHIP Extension Act of 2007, as modified by the American Recovery and Reinvestment Act, to extend for two years: (1) certain payment rules for long-term care hospital services; and (2) a certain moratorium on the establishment of certain hospitals and facilities.

(Sec. 3107) Amends MIPPA to extend the physician fee schedule mental health add-on payment provision through December 31, 2010.

(Sec. 3108) Allows a physician assistant who does not have an employment relationship with a SNF, but who is working in collaboration with a physician, to certify the need for post-hospital extended care services for Medicare payment purposes.

(Sec. 3109) Amends title XVIII, as modified by MIPPA, to exempt certain pharmacies from accreditation requirements until the Secretary develops pharmacy-specific standards.

(Sec. 3110) Creates a special Part B enrollment period for military retirees, their spouses (including widows/widowers), and dependent children, who are otherwise eligible for TRICARE (the health care plan under the Department of Defense [DOD]) and entitled to Medicare Part A (Hospital Insurance) based on disability or end stage renal disease, but who have declined Medicare Part B (Supplementary Medical Insurance).

(Sec. 3111) Sets payments for dual-energy x-ray absorptiometry services in 2010 and 2011 at 70% of the 2006 reimbursement rates. Directs the Secretary to arrange with the Institute of Medicine of the National Academies to study and report to the Secretary and Congress on the ramifications of Medicare reimbursement reductions for such services on beneficiary access to bone mass measurement benefits.

(Sec. 3112) Eliminates funding in the Medicare Improvement Fund FY2014.

(Sec. 3113) Directs the Secretary to conduct a demonstration project under Medicare Part B of separate payments for complex diagnostic laboratory tests provided to individuals.

(Sec. 3114) Increases from 65% to 100% of the fee schedule amount provided for the same service performed by a physician the fee schedule for certified-midwife services provided on or after January 1, 2011.

Part II: Rural Protections

(Sec. 3121) Extends through 2010 hold harmless provisions under the prospective payment system for hospital outpatient department services.

Removes the 100-bed limitation for sole community hospitals so all such hospitals receive an 85% increase in the payment difference in 2010.

(Sec. 3122) Amends the Medicare Prescription Drug, Improvement, and Modernization Act of 2003, as modified by other federal law, to extend from July 1, 2010, until July 1, 2011, the reasonable cost reimbursement for clinical diagnostic laboratory service for qualifying rural hospitals with under 50 beds.

(Sec. 3123, as modified by Sec. 10313) Extends the Rural Community Hospital Demonstration Program for five additional years. Expands the maximum number of participating hospitals to 30, and to 20 the number of demonstration states with low population densities.

(Sec. 3124) Extends the Medicare-dependent Hospital Program through FY2012.

(Sec. 3125, as modified by Sec. 10314) Modifies the Medicare inpatient hospital payment adjustment for low-volume hospitals for FY2011-FY2012.

(Sec. 3126) Revises requirements for the Demonstration Project on Community Health Integration Models in Certain Rural Counties to allow additional counties as well as physicians to participate.

(Sec. 3127) Directs MEDPAC to study and report to Congress on the adequacy of payments for items and services furnished by service providers and suppliers in rural areas under the Medicare program.

(Sec. 3128) Allows a critical access hospital to continue to be eligible to receive 101% of reasonable costs for providing: (1) outpatient care regardless of the eligible billing method such hospital uses; and (2) qualifying ambulance services.

(Sec. 3129) Extends through FY2012 FLEX grants under the Medicare Rural Hospital Flexibility Program. Allows the use of grant funding to assist small rural hospitals to participate in delivery system reforms.

Part III: Improving Payment Accuracy

(Sec. 3131, as modified by Sec. 10315) Requires the Secretary, starting in 2014, to rebase home health payments by an appropriate percentage, among other things, to reflect the number, mix, and level of intensity of home health services in an episode, and the average cost of providing care.

Directs the Secretary to study and report to Congress on home health agency costs involved with providing ongoing access to care to low-income Medicare beneficiaries or beneficiaries in medically underserved areas, and in treating beneficiaries with varying levels of severity of illness. Authorizes a Medicare demonstration project based on the study results.

(Sec. 3132) Requires the Secretary, by January 1, 2011, to begin collecting additional data and information needed to revise payments for hospice care.

Directs the Secretary, not earlier than October 1, 2013, to implement, by regulation, budget neutral revisions to the methodology for determining hospice payments for routine home care and other services, which may include per diem payments reflecting changes in resource intensity in providing such care and services during the course of an entire episode of hospice care.

Requires the Secretary to impose new requirements on hospice providers participating in Medicare, including requirements for: (1) a hospice physician or nurse practitioner to have a face-to-face encounter with the individual regarding eligibility and recertification; and (2) a medical review of any stays exceeding 180 days, where the number of such cases exceeds a specified percentage of them for all hospice programs.

(Sec. 3133, as modified by Sec. 10316) Specifies reductions to Medicare DSH payments for FY2015 and ensuing fiscal years, especially to subsection (d) hospitals, to reflect lower uncompensated care costs relative to increases in the number of insured. (Generally, a subsection [d] hospital is an acute care hospital, particularly one that receives payments under Medicare's inpatient prospective payment system when providing covered inpatient services to eligible beneficiaries.)

(Sec. 3134) Directs the Secretary periodically to identify physician services as being potentially misvalued and make appropriate adjustments to the relative values of such services under the Medicare physician fee schedule.

(Sec. 3135) Increases the presumed utilization rate for calculating the payment for advanced imaging equipment other than low-tech imaging such as ultrasound, x-rays and EKGs.

Increases the technical component payment "discount" for sequential imaging services on contiguous body parts during the same visit.

(Sec. 3136) Restricts the lump-sum payment option for new or replacement chairs to the complex, rehabilitative power-driven wheelchairs only. Eliminates the lump-sum payment option for all other power-driven wheelchairs. Makes the rental payment for power-driven wheelchairs 15% of the purchase price for each of the first three months (instead of 10%), and 6% of the purchase price for each of the remaining 10 months of the rental period (instead of 7.5%).

(Sec. 3137, as modified by Sec. 10317) Amends the Tax Relief and Health Care Act of 2006, as modified by other federal law, to extend "Section 508" hospital reclassifications until September 30, 2010, with a special rule for FY2010. ("Section 508" refers to Section 508 of the Medicare Modernization Act of 2003, which allows the temporary reclassification of a hospital with a low Medicare area wage index, for reimbursement purposes, to a nearby location with a higher Medicare area wage index, so that the "Section 508 hospital" will receive the higher Medicare reimbursement rate.)

Directs the Secretary to report to Congress a plan to reform the hospital wage index system.

(Sec. 3138) Requires the Secretary to determine if the outpatient costs incurred by inpatient prospective payment system-exempt cancer hospitals, including those for drugs and biologicals, with respect to Medicare ambulatory payment classification groups, exceed those costs incurred by other hospitals reimbursed under the outpatient prospective payment system (OPPS). Requires the Secretary, if this is so, to provide for an appropriate OPPS adjustment to reflect such higher costs for services furnished on or after January 1, 2011.

(Sec. 3139) Allows a biosimilar biological product to be reimbursed at 6% of the average sales price of the brand biological product.

(Sec. 3140) Directs the Secretary to establish a Medicare Hospice Concurrent Care demonstration program under which Medicare beneficiaries are furnished, during the same period, hospice care and any other Medicare items or services from Medicare funds otherwise paid to such hospice programs.

(Sec. 3141) Requires application of the budget neutrality requirement associated with the effect of the imputed rural floor on the area wage index under the Balanced Budget Act of 1997 through a uniform national, instead of state-by-state, adjustment to the area hospital wage index floor.

(Sec. 3142) Directs the Secretary to study and report to Congress on the need for an additional payment for urban Medicare-dependent hospitals for inpatient hospital services under Medicare.

(Sec. 3143) Declares that nothing in this Act shall result in the reduction of guaranteed home health benefits under the Medicare program.

Subtitle C: Provisions Relating to Part C

(Sec. 3201, as modified by Sec. 10318) Bases the MedicareAdvantage (MA) benchmark on the average of the bids from MA plans in each market.

Revises the formula for calculating the annual Medicare+Choice capitation rate to reduce the national MA per capita Medicare+Choice growth percentage used to increase benchmarks in 2011.

Increases the monthly MA plan rebates from 75% to 100% of the average per capita savings.

Requires that bid information which MA plans are required to submit to the Secretary be certified by a member of the American Academy of Actuaries and meet actuarial guidelines and rules established by the Secretary.

Directs the Secretary, acting through the CMS Chief Actuary, to establish actuarial guidelines for the submission of bid information and bidding rules that are appropriate to ensure accurate bids and fair competition among MA plans.

Directs the Secretary to: (1) establish new MA payment areas for urban areas based on the Core Based Statistical Area; and (2) make monthly care coordination and management performance bonus payments, quality performance bonus payments, and quality bonuses for new and low enrollment MA plans, to MA plans that meet certain criteria.

Directs the Secretary to provide transitional rebates for the provision of extra benefits to enrollees.

(Sec. 3202) Prohibits MA plans from charging beneficiaries cost sharing for chemotherapy administration services, renal dialysis services, or skilled nursing care that is greater than what is charged under the traditional fee-for-service program.

Requires MA plans to apply the full amount of rebates, bonuses, and supplemental premiums according to the following order: (1) reduction of cost sharing, (2) coverage of preventive care and wellness benefits, and (3) other benefits not covered under the original Medicare fee-for-service program.

(Sec. 3203) Requires the Secretary to analyze the differences in coding patterns between MA and the original Medicare fee-for-service programs. Authorizes the Secretary to incorporate the results of the analysis into risk scores for 2014 and subsequent years.

(Sec. 3204) Allows beneficiaries to disenroll from an MA plan and return to the traditional Medicare fee-for-service program from January 1 to March 15 of each year.

Revises requirements for annual beneficiary election periods.

(Sec. 3205) Amends SSA title XVIII (Medicare), as modified by MIPPA, to extend special needs plan (SNP) authority through December 31, 2013.

Authorizes the Secretary to establish a frailty payment adjustment under PACE payment rules for fully-integrated, dual-eligible SNPs.

Extends authority through calendar 2012 for SNPs that do not have contracts with state Medicaid programs to continue to operate, but not to expand their service areas.

Directs the Secretary to require an MA organization offering a specialized MA plan for special needs individuals to be approved by the National Committee for Quality Assurance.

Requires the Secretary to use a risk score reflecting the known underlying risk profile and chronic health status of similar individuals, instead of the default risk score, for new enrollees in MA plans that are not specialized MA SNPs.

(Sec. 3206) Extends through calendar 2012 the length of time reasonable cost plans may continue operating regardless of any other MA plans serving the area.

(Sec. 3208) Creates a new type of MA plan called an MA Senior Housing Facility Plan, which would be allowed to limit its service area to a senior housing facility (continuing care retirement community) within a geographic area.

(Sec. 3209) Declares that the Secretary is not required to accept any or every bid submitted by an MA plan or Medicare Part D prescription drug plan that proposes to increase significantly any beneficiary cost sharing or decrease benefits offered.

(Sec. 3210) Directs the Secretary to request the National Association of Insurance Commissioners (NAIC) to develop new standards for certain Medigap plans.

Subtitle D: Medicare Part D Improvements for Prescription Drug Plans and MA-PD Plans

(Sec. 3301) Amends Medicare Part D (Voluntary Prescription Drug Benefit Program) to establish conditions for the availability of coverage for Part D drugs. Requires the manufacturer to participate in the Medicare coverage gap discount program.

Directs the Secretary to establish such a program.

(Sec. 3302) Excludes the MA rebate amounts and quality bonus payments from calculation of the regional low-income subsidy benchmark premium for MA monthly prescription drug beneficiaries.

(Sec. 3303) Directs the Secretary to permit a prescription drug plan or an MA-PD plan to waive the monthly beneficiary premium for a subsidy eligible individual if the amount of such premium is *de minimis*. Provides that, if such premium is waived, the Secretary shall not reassign subsidy eligible individuals enrolled in the plan to other plans based on the fact that the monthly beneficiary premium under the plan was greater than the low-income benchmark premium amount.

Authorizes the Secretary to auto-enroll subsidy eligible individuals in plans that waive *de minimis* premiums.

(Sec. 3304) Sets forth a special rule for widows and widowers regarding eligibility for low-income assistance. Allows the surviving spouse of an eligible couple to delay redetermination of eligibility for one year after the death of a spouse.

(Sec. 3305) Directs the Secretary, in the case of a subsidy eligible individual enrolled in one prescription drug plan but subsequently reassigned by the Secretary to a new prescription drug plan, to provide the individual with: (1) information on formulary differences between the individual's former plan and the new plan with respect to the individual's drug regimens; and (2) a description of the individual's right to request a coverage determination, exception, or reconsideration, bring an appeal, or resolve a grievance.

(Sec. 3306) Amends MIPPA to provide additional funding for FY2010-FY2012 for outreach and education activities related to specified Medicare low-income assistance programs.

(Sec. 3307) Authorizes the Secretary to identify classes of clinical concern through rulemaking, including anticonvulsants, antidepressants, antineoplastics, antipsychotics, antiretrovirals, and immunosuppressants for the treatment of transplant rejection. Requires prescription drug plan sponsors to include all drugs in these classes in their formularies.

(Sec. 3308) Requires Part D enrollees who exceed certain income thresholds to pay higher premiums. Revises the current authority of the IRS to disclose income information to the Social Security Administration for purposes of adjusting the Part B subsidy.

(Sec. 3309) Eliminates cost sharing for certain dual eligible individuals receiving care under a home and community-based waiver program who would otherwise require institutional care.

(Sec. 3310) Directs the Secretary to require sponsors of prescription drug plans to utilize specific, uniform techniques for dispensing covered Part D drugs to enrollees who reside in a long-term care facility in order to reduce waste associated with 30-day refills.

(Sec. 3311) Directs the Secretary to develop and maintain an easy-to-use complaint system to collect and maintain information on MA-PD plan and prescription drug complaints received by the Secretary until the complaint is resolved.

(Sec. 3312) Requires a prescription drug plan sponsor to: (1) use a single, uniform exceptions and appeals process for determination of a plan enrollee's prescription drug coverage; and (2) provide instant access to this process through a toll-free telephone number and an Internet website.

(Sec. 3313) Requires the HHS Inspector General to study and report to Congress on the inclusion in formularies of: (1) drugs commonly used by dual eligibles; and (2) prescription drug prices under Medicare Part D and Medicaid.

(Sec. 3314) Allows the costs incurred by AIDS drug assistance programs and by IHS in providing prescription drugs to count toward the annual out-of-pocket threshold.

(Sec. 3315) Increases by $500 the 2010 standard initial coverage limit (thus decreasing the time that a Part D enrollee would be in the coverage gap).

Subtitle E: Ensuring Medicare Sustainability

(Sec. 3401, as modified by Sec. 10319 and Sec. 10322) Revises certain market basket updates and incorporates a full productivity adjustment into any updates that do not already incorporate such adjustments, including inpatient hospitals, home health providers, nursing homes, hospice providers, inpatient psychiatric facilities, long-term care hospitals, inpatient rehabilitation facilities, and Part B providers.

Establishes a quality measure reporting program for psychiatric hospitals beginning in FY2014.

(Sec. 3402) Revises requirements for reduction of the Medicare Part B premium subsidy based on income. Maintains the current 2010 income thresholds for the period of 2011 through 2019.

(Sec. 3403, as modified by Sec. 10320) Establishes an Independent Payment Advisory Board to develop and submit detailed proposals to reduce the per capita rate of growth in Medicare spending to the President for Congress to consider. Establishes a consumer advisory council to advise the Board on the impact of payment policies under this title on consumers.

Subtitle F: Health Care Quality Improvements

(Sec. 3501) Amends the Public Health Service Act to direct the Center for Quality Improvement and Patient Safety of the Agency for Healthcare Research and Quality (AHRQ) to conduct or support activities for best practices in the delivery of health care services and support research on the development of tools to facilitate adoption of best practices that improve the quality, safety, and efficiency of health care delivery services. Authorizes appropriations for FY2010-FY2014.

Requires the AHRQ Director, through the AHRQ Center for Quality Improvement and Patient Safety, to award grants or contracts to eligible entities to provide technical support or to implement models and practices identified in the research conducted by the Center.

(Sec. 3502, as modified by Sec. 10321) Directs the Secretary to establish a program to provide grants to or enter into contracts with eligible entities to establish community-based interdisciplinary, interprofessional teams to support primary care practices, including obstetrics and gynecology practices, within the hospital service areas served by the eligible entities.

(Sec. 3503) Directs the Secretary, acting through the Patient Safety Research Center, to establish a program to provide grants or contracts to eligible entities to implement medication management services provided by licensed pharmacists, as a collaborative multidisciplinary, inter-professional approach to the treatment of chronic diseases for targeted individuals, to improve the quality of care and reduce overall cost in the treatment of such disease.

(Sec. 3504) Directs the Secretary, acting through the Assistant Secretary for Preparedness and Response, to award at least four multiyear contracts or competitive grants to eligible entities to support pilot projects that design, implement, and evaluate innovative models of regionalized, comprehensive, and accountable emergency care and trauma systems.

Requires the Secretary to support federal programs administered by the National Institutes of Health (NIH), the AHRQ, the Health Resources and Services Administration (HRSA), the CMS, and other agencies involved in improving the emergency care system to expand and accelerate research in emergency medical care systems and emergency medicine.

Directs the Secretary to support federal programs administered by such agencies to coordinate and expand research in pediatric emergency medical care systems and pediatric emergency medicine.

Authorizes appropriations for FY2010-FY2014.

(Sec. 3505) Requires the Secretary to establish three programs to award grants to qualified public, nonprofit IHS, Indian tribal, and urban Indian trauma centers to: (1) assist in defraying substantial uncompensated care costs; (2) further the core missions of such trauma centers, including by addressing costs associated with patient stabilization and transfer; and (3) provide emergency relief to ensure the continued and future availability of trauma services. Authorizes appropriations for FY2010-FY2015.

Directs the Secretary to provide funding to states to enable them to award grants to eligible entities for trauma services. Authorizes appropriations for FY2010-FY2015.

(Sec. 3506) Directs the Secretary to: (1) establish a program to award grants or contracts to develop, update, and produce patient decision aids to assist health care providers and patients; (2) establish a program to provide for the phased-in development, implementation, and evaluation of shared decision making using patient decision aids to meet the objective of improving the understanding of patients of their medical treatment options; and (3) award grants for establishment and support of Shared Decisionmaking Resource Centers. Authorizes appropriations for FY2010 and subsequent fiscal years.

(Sec. 3507) Requires the Secretary, acting through the Commissioner of Food and Drugs, to determine whether the addition of quantitative summaries of the benefits and risks of prescription drugs in a standardized format to the promotional labeling or print advertising of such drugs would improve heath care decisionmaking by clinicians and patients and consumers.

(Sec. 3508) Authorizes the Secretary to award grants to eligible entities or consortia to carry out demonstration projects to develop and implement academic curricula that integrate quality improvement and patient safety in the clinical education of health professionals.

(Sec. 3509) Establishes an Office on Women's Health within the Office of the Secretary, the Office of the Director of the Centers for Disease Control and Prevention (CDC), the Office of the AHRQ Director, the Office of the Administrator of HRSA, and the Office of the Commissioner of Food and Drugs.

Authorizes appropriations for FY2010-FY2014 for all such Offices on Women's Health.

(Sec. 3510) Extends from three years to four years the duration of a patient navigator grant.

Prohibits the Secretary from awarding such a grant unless the recipient entity provides assurances that patient navigators recruited, assigned, trained, or employed using grant funds meet minimum core proficiencies tailored for the main focus or intervention of the navigator involved.

Authorizes appropriations for FY2010-FY2015.

(Sec. 3511) Authorizes appropriations to carry out this title, except where otherwise provided in the title.

(Sec. 3512, as added by Sec. 10201) Directs the Comptroller General to study and report to Congress on whether the development, recognition, or implementation of any guideline or other standards under specified provisions of this Act would result in the establishment of a new cause of action or claim.

Subtitle G: *Protecting and Improving Guaranteed Medicare Benefits*

(Sec. 3601) Provides that nothing in this Act shall result in a reduction of guaranteed benefits under the Medicare program.

States that savings generated for the Medicare program under this Act shall extend the solvency of the Medicare trust funds, reduce Medicare premiums and other cost-sharing for beneficiaries, and improve or expand guaranteed Medicare benefits and protect access to Medicare providers.

(Sec. 3602) Declares that nothing in this Act shall result in the reduction or elimination of any benefits guaranteed by law to participants in MA plans.

Title IV: Prevention of Chronic Disease and Improving Public Health

Subtitle A: *Modernizing Disease Prevention and Public Health Systems*

(Sec. 4001, as modified by Sec. 10401) Requires the President to: (1) establish the National Prevention, Health Promotion and Public Health Council; (2) establish the Advisory Group on Prevention, Health Promotion, and Integrative and Public Health; and (3) appoint the Surgeon General as Chairperson of the Council in order to develop a national prevention, health promotion, and public health strategy.

Requires the Secretary and the Comptroller General to conduct periodic reviews and evaluations of every federal disease prevention and health promotion initiative, program, and agency.

(Sec. 4002, as modified by Sec. 10401) Establishes a Prevention and Public Health Fund to provide for expanded and sustained national investment in prevention and public health programs to improve health and help restrain the rate of growth in private and public sector health care costs. Authorizes appropriations and appropriates money to such Fund.

(Sec 4003) Requires (currently, allows) the Director of AHRQ to convene the Preventive Services Task Force to review scientific evidence related to the effectiveness, appropriateness, and cost-effectiveness of clinical preventive services for the purpose of developing recommendations for the health care community.

Requires the Director of CDC to convene an independent Community Preventive Services Task Force to review scientific evidence related to the effectiveness, appropriateness, and cost-effectiveness of community preventive interventions for the purpose of developing recommendations for individuals and organizations delivering populations-based services and other policy makers.

(Sec. 4004, as modified by Sec. 10401) Requires the Secretary to provide for the planning and implementation of a national public-private partnership for a prevention and health promotion outreach and education campaign to raise public awareness of health improvement across the life span.

Requires the Secretary, acting through the Director of CDC, to: (1) establish and implement a national science-based media campaign on health promotion and disease prevention; and (2) enter into a contract for the development and operation of a federal website personalized prevention plan tool.

Subtitle B: Increasing Access to Clinical Preventive Services

(Sec. 4101, as modified by Sec. 10402) Requires the Secretary to establish a program to award grants to eligible entities to support the operation of school-based health centers.

(Sec. 4102) Requires the Secretary, acting through the Director of CDC, to carry out oral health activities, including: (1) establishing a national public education campaign that is focused on oral health care prevention and education; (2) awarding demonstration grants for research-based dental caries disease management activities; (3) awarding grants for the development of school-based dental sealant programs; and (4) entering into cooperative agreements with state, territorial, and Indian tribes or tribal organizations for oral health data collection and interpretation, a delivery system for oral health, and science-based programs to improve oral health.

Requires the Secretary to: (1) update and improve the Pregnancy Risk Assessment Monitoring System as it relates to oral health care; (2) develop oral health care components for inclusion in the National Health and Nutrition Examination Survey; and (3) ensure that the Medical Expenditures Panel Survey by AHRQ includes the verification of dental utilization, expenditure, and coverage findings through conduct of a look-back analysis.

(Sec. 4103, as modified by Sec. 10402) Amends SSA title XVIII (Medicare) to provide coverage of personalized prevention plan services, including a health risk assessment, for individuals. Prohibits cost-sharing for such services.

(Sec. 4104, as modified by Sec. 10406) Eliminates cost-sharing for certain preventive services recommended by the United States Preventive Services Task Force.

(Sec. 4105) Authorizes the Secretary to modify Medicare coverage of any preventive service consistent with the recommendations of such Task Force.

(Sec. 4106) Amends SSA title XIX (Medicaid) to provide Medicaid coverage of preventive services and approved vaccines. Increases the FMAP for such services and vaccines.

(Sec. 4107) Provides for Medicaid coverage of counseling and pharmacotherapy for cessation of tobacco use by pregnant women.

(Sec. 4108) Requires the Secretary to award grants to states to carry out initiatives to provide incentives to Medicaid beneficiaries who participate in programs to lower health risk and demonstrate changes in health risk and outcomes.

Subtitle C: Creating Healthier Communities

(Sec. 4201, as modified by Sec. 10403) Requires the Secretary, acting through the Director of CDC, to award grants to state and local governmental agencies and community-based organizations for the implementation, evaluation, and dissemination of evidence-based community preventive health activities in order to reduce chronic disease rates, prevent the development of secondary conditions, address health disparities, and develop a stronger evidence base of effective prevention programming.

(Sec. 4202) Requires the Secretary, acting through the Director of CDC, to award grants to state or local health departments and Indian tribes to carry out pilot programs to provide public health community interventions, screenings, and clinical referrals for individuals who are between 55 and 64 years of age.

Requires the Secretary to: (1) conduct an evaluation of community-based prevention and wellness programs and develop a plan for promoting healthy lifestyles and chronic disease self-management for Medicare beneficiaries; and (2) evaluate community prevention and wellness programs that have demonstrated potential to help Medicare beneficiaries reduce their risk of disease, disability, and injury by making healthy lifestyle choices.

(Sec. 4203) Amends the Rehabilitation Act of 1973 to require the Architectural and Transportation Barriers Compliance Board to promulgate standards setting forth the minimum technical criteria for medical diagnostic equipment used in medical settings to ensure that such equipment is accessible to, and usable by, individuals with accessibility needs.

(Sec. 4204) Authorizes the Secretary to negotiate and enter into contracts with vaccine manufacturers for the purchase and delivery of vaccines for adults. Allows a state to purchase additional quantities of adult vaccines from manufacturers at the applicable price negotiated by the Secretary. Requires the Secretary, acting through the Director of CDC, to establish a demonstration program to award grants to states to improve the provision of recommended immunizations for children and adults through the use of evidence-based, population-based interventions for high-risk populations.

Reauthorizes appropriations for preventive health service programs to immunize children and adults against vaccine-preventable diseases without charge.

Requires the Comptroller General to study the ability of Medicare beneficiaries who are 65 years or older to access routinely recommended vaccines covered under the prescription drug program since its establishment.

(Sec. 4205) Amends the Federal Food, Drug, and Cosmetic Act to require the labeling of a food item offered for sale in a retail food establishment that is part of a chain with 20 or more locations under the same name to disclose on the menu and menu board: (1) the number of calories contained in the standard menu item; (2) the suggested daily caloric intake; and (3) the availability on the premises and upon request of specified additional nutrient information. Requires self-service facilities to place adjacent to each food offered a sign that lists calories per displayed food item or per serving. Requires vending machine operators who operate 20 or more vending machines to provide a sign disclosing the number of calories contained in each article of food.

(Sec. 4206) Requires the Secretary to establish a pilot program to test the impact of providing at-risk populations who utilize community health centers an individualized wellness plan designed to reduce risk factors for preventable conditions as identified by a comprehensive risk-factor assessment.

(Sec. 4207) Amends the Fair Labor Standards Act of 1938 to require employers to provide a reasonable break time and a suitable place, other than a bathroom, for an employee to express breast milk for her nursing child. Excludes an employer with fewer than 50 employees if such requirements would impose an undue hardship.

Subtitle D: Support for Prevention and Public Health Innovation

(Sec. 4301) Requires the Secretary, acting through the Director of CDC, to provide funding for research in the area of public health services and systems.

(Sec. 4302) Requires the Secretary to ensure that any federally conducted or supported health care or public health program, activity, or survey collects and reports specified demographic data regarding health disparities.

Requires the Secretary, acting through the National Coordinator for Health Information Technology, to develop: (1) national standards for the management of data collected; and (2) interoperability and security systems for data management.

(Sec. 4303, as modified by Sec. 10404) Requires the Director of CDC to: (1) provide employers with technical assistance, consultation, tools, and other resources in evaluating employer-based wellness programs; and (2) build evaluation capacity among workplace staff by training employers on how to evaluate such wellness programs and ensuring that evaluation resources, technical assistance, and consultation are available.

Requires the Director of CDC to conduct a national worksite health policies and programs survey to assess employer-based health policies and programs.

(Sec. 4304) Requires the Secretary, acting through the Director of CDC, to establish an Epidemiology and Laboratory Capacity Grant Program to award grants to assist public health agencies in improving surveillance for, and response to, infectious diseases and other conditions of public health importance.

(Sec. 4305) Requires the Secretary to: (1) enter into an agreement with the Institute of Medicine to convene a Conference on Pain, the purposes of which shall include to increase the recognition of pain as a significant public health problem in the United States; and (2) establish the Interagency Pain Research Coordinating Committee.

(Sec. 4306) Appropriates funds to carry out childhood obesity demonstration projects.

Subtitle E: Miscellaneous Provisions

(Sec. 4402) Requires the Secretary to evaluate programs to determine whether existing federal health and wellness initiatives are effective in achieving their stated goals.

Title V: Health Care Workforce

Subtitle A: Purpose and Definitions

(Sec. 5001) Declares that the purpose of this title is to improve access to and the delivery of health care services for all individuals, particularly low-income, underserved, uninsured, minority, health disparity, and rural populations.

Subtitle B: Innovations in the Health Care Workforce

(Sec. 5101, as modified by Sec. 10501) Establishes a National Health Care Workforce Commission to: (1) review current and projected health care workforce supply and demand; and (2) make recommendations to Congress and the Administration concerning national health care workforce priorities, goals, and policies.

(Sec. 5102) Establishes a health care workforce development grant program.

(Sec. 5103) Requires the Secretary to establish the National Center for Health Care Workforce Analysis to provide for the development of information describing and analyzing the health care workforce and workforce related issues. Transfers the responsibilities and resources of the National Center for Health Workforce Analysis to the Center created under this section.

(Sec. 5104, as added by Sec. 10501) Establishes the Interagency Access to Health Care in Alaska Task Force to: (1) assess access to health care for beneficiaries of federal health care systems in Alaska; and (2) develop a strategy to improve delivery to such beneficiaries.

Subtitle C: Increasing the Supply of the Health Care Workforce

(Sec. 5201) Revises student loan repayment provisions related to the length of service requirement for the primary health care loan repayment program.

(Sec. 5202) Increases maximum amount of loans made by schools of nursing to students.

(Sec. 5203) Directs the Secretary to establish and carry out a pediatric specialty loan repayment program.

(Sec. 5204) Requires the Secretary to establish the Public Health Workforce Loan Repayment Program to assure an adequate supply of public health professionals to eliminate critical public health workforce shortages in federal, state, local, and tribal public health agencies.

(Sec. 5205) Amends the Higher Education Act of 1965 to expand student loan forgiveness to include allied health professionals employed in public health agencies.

(Sec. 5206) Includes public health workforce loan repayment programs as permitted activities under a grant program to increase the number of individuals in the public health workforce.

Authorizes the Secretary to provide for scholarships for mid-career professionals in the public health and allied health workforce to receive additional training in the field of public health and allied health.

(Sec. 5207) Authorizes appropriations for the National Health Service Corps Scholarship Program and the National Health Service Corps Loan Repayment Program.

(Sec. 5208) Requires the Secretary to award grants for the cost of the operation of nurse-managed health clinics.

(Sec. 5209) Eliminates the cap on the number of commissioned officers in the Public Health Service Regular Corps.

(Sec. 5210) Revises the Regular Corps and the Reserve Corps (renamed the Ready Reserve Corps) in the Public Health Service. Sets forth the uses of the Ready Reserve Corps.

Subtitle D: Enhancing Health Care Workforce Education and Training

(Sec. 5301) Sets forth provisions providing for health care professional training programs.

(Sec. 5302) Requires the Secretary to award grants for new training opportunities for direct care workers who are employed in long-term care settings.

(Sec. 5303) Sets forth provisions providing for dentistry professional training programs.

(Sec. 5304) Authorizes the Secretary to award grants for demonstration programs to establish training programs for alternative dental health care providers in order to increase access to dental health services in rural and other underserved communities.

(Sec. 5305) Requires the Secretary to award grants or contracts to entities that operate a geriatric education center to offer short-term, intensive courses that focus on geriatrics, chronic care management, and long-term care.

Expands geriatric faculty fellowship programs to make dentists eligible.

Reauthorizes and revises the geriatric education programs to allow grant funds to be used for the establishment of traineeships for individuals who are preparing for advanced education nursing degrees in areas that specialize in the care of elderly populations.

(Sec. 5306) Authorizes the Secretary to award grants to institutions of higher education to support the recruitment of students for, and education and clinical experience of the students in, social work programs, psychology programs, child and adolescent mental health, and training of paraprofessional child and adolescent mental health workers.

(Sec. 5307) Authorizes the Secretary, acting through the Administrator of HRSA, to award grants, contracts, or cooperative agreements for the development, evaluation, and dissemination of research, demonstration projects, and model curricula for health professions training in cultural competency, prevention, public health proficiency, reducing health disparities, and working with individuals with disabilities.

(Sec. 5308) Requires nurse-midwifery programs, in order to be eligible for advanced education nursing grants, to have as their objective the education of midwives and to be accredited by the American College of Nurse-Midwives Accreditation Commission for Midwifery Education.

(Sec. 5309) Authorizes the Secretary to award grants or enter into contracts to enhance the nursing workforce by initiating and maintaining nurse retention programs.

(Sec. 5310) Makes nurse faculty at an accredited school of nursing eligible for the nursing education loan repayment program.

(Sec. 5311) Revises the nurse faculty loan repayment program, including to increase the amount of such loans.

Authorizes the Secretary, acting through the Administrator of HRSA, to enter into an agreement for the repayment of education loans in exchange for service as a member of a faculty at an accredited school of nursing.

(Sec. 5312) Authorizes appropriations for carrying out nursing workforce programs.

(Sec. 5313, as modified by Sec. 10501) Requires the Director of CDC to award grants to eligible entities to promote positive health behaviors and outcomes for populations in medically underserved communities through the use of community health workers.

(Sec. 5314) Authorizes the Secretary to carry out activities to address documented workforce shortages in state and local health departments in the critical areas of applied public health epidemiology and public health laboratory science and informatics.

(Sec. 5315) Authorizes the establishment of the United States Public Health Sciences Track, which is authorized to award advanced degrees in public health, epidemiology, and emergency preparedness and response.

Directs the Surgeon General to develop: (1) an integrated longitudinal plan for health professions continuing education; and (2) faculty development programs and curricula in decentralized venues of health care to balance urban, tertiary, and inpatient venues.

(Sec. 5316, as added by Sec. 10501) Requires the Secretary to establish a training demonstration program for family nurse practitioners to employ and provide one-year training for nurse practitioners serving as primary care providers in federally qualified health centers or nurse-managed health centers.

Subtitle E: Supporting the Existing Health Care Workforce

(Sec. 5401) Revises the allocation of funds to assist schools in supporting programs of excellence in health professions education for underrepresented minority individuals and schools designated as centers of excellence.

(Sec. 5402, as modified by Sec. 10501) Makes schools offering physician assistant education programs eligible for loan repayment for health profession faculty. Increases the amount of loan repayment for such programs.

Authorizes appropriations for: (1) scholarships for disadvantaged students attending health professions or nursing schools; (2) loan repayment for health professions faculty; and (3) grants to health professions schools to assist individuals from disadvantaged backgrounds.

(Sec. 5403) Requires the Secretary to: (1) make awards for area health education center programs; and (2) provide for timely dissemination of research findings using relevant resources.

(Sec. 5404) Makes revisions to the grant program to increase nursing education opportunities for individuals from disadvantaged backgrounds to include providing: (1) stipends for diploma or associate degree nurses to enter a bridge or degree completion program; (2) student scholarships or stipends for accelerated nursing degree programs; and (3) advanced education preparation.

(Sec. 5405, as modified by Sec. 10501) Requires the Secretary, acting through the Director of AHRQ, to establish a Primary Care Extension Program to provide support and assistance to educate primary care providers about preventive medicine, health promotion, chronic disease management, mental and behavioral health services, and evidence-based and evidence-informed therapies and techniques.

Requires the Secretary to award grants to states for the establishment of Primary Care Extension Program State Hubs to coordinate state health care functions with quality improvement organizations and area health education centers.

Subtitle F: Strengthening Primary Care and Other Workforce Improvements

(Sec. 5501, as modified by Sec. 10501) Requires Medicare incentive payments to: (1) primary care practitioners providing primary care services on or after January 1, 2011, and before January 1, 2016; and (2) general surgeons performing major surgical procedures on or after January 1, 2011, and before January 1, 2016, in a health professional shortage area.

(Sec. 5502, deleted by Sec. 10501)

(Sec. 5503) Reallocates unused residency positions to qualifying hospitals for primary care residents for purposes of payments to hospitals for graduate medical education costs.

(Sec. 5504) Revises provisions related to graduate medical education costs to count the time residents spend in nonprovider settings toward the full-time equivalency if the hospital incurs the costs of the stipends and fringe benefits of such residents during such time.

(Sec. 5505, as modified by Sec. 10501) Includes toward the determination of full-time equivalency for graduate medical education costs time spent by an intern or resident in an approved medical residency training program in a nonprovider setting that is primarily engaged in furnishing patient care in nonpatient care activities.

(Sec. 5506) Directs the Secretary, when a hospital with an approved medical residency program closes, to increase the resident limit for other hospitals based on proximity criteria.

(Sec. 5507) Requires the Secretary to: (1) award grants for demonstration projects that are designed to provide certain low-income individuals with the opportunity to obtain education and training for health care occupations that pay well and that are expected to experience labor shortages or be in high demand; and (2) award grants to states to conduct demonstration projects for purposes of developing core training competencies and certification programs for personal or home care aides.

Authorizes appropriations for FY2009-FY2012 for family-to-family health information centers.

(Sec. 5508) Authorizes the Secretary to award grants to teaching health centers for the purpose of establishing new accredited or expanded primary care residency programs.

Allows up to 50% of time spent teaching by a member of the National Health Service Corps to be considered clinical practice for purposes of fulfilling the service obligation.

Requires the Secretary to make payments for direct and indirect expenses to qualified teaching health centers for expansion or establishment of approved graduate medical residency training programs.

(Sec. 5509) Requires the Secretary to establish a graduate nurse education demonstration under which a hospital may receive payment for the hospital's reasonable costs for the provision of qualified clinical training to advance practice nurses.

Subtitle G: Improving Access to Health Care Services

(Sec. 5601) Reauthorizes appropriations for health centers to serve medically underserved populations.

(Sec. 5602) Requires the Secretary to establish through the negotiated rulemaking process a comprehensive methodology and criteria for designation of medically underserved populations and health professions shortage areas.

(Sec. 5603) Reauthorizes appropriations for FY2010-FY2014 for the expansion and improvement of emergency medical services for children who need treatment for trauma or critical care.

(Sec. 5604) Authorizes the Secretary, acting through the Administrator of the Substance Abuse and Mental Health Services Administration, to award grants and cooperative agreements for demonstration projects for the provision of coordinated and integrated services to special populations through the co-location of primary and specialty care services in community-based mental and behavioral health settings.

(Sec. 5605) Establishes a Commission on Key National Indicators to: (1) conduct comprehensive oversight of a newly established key national indicators system; and (2) make recommendations on how to improve such system. Directs the National Academy of Sciences to enable the establishment of such system by creating its own institutional capability or by partnering with an independent private nonprofit organization to implement such system. Directs the Comptroller General to study previous work conducted by all public agencies, private organizations, or foreign countries with respect to best practices for such systems.

(Sec. 5606, as added by Sec. 10501) Authorizes a state to award grants to health care providers who treat a high percentage of medically underserved populations or other special populations in the state.

Subtitle H: General Provisions

(Sec. 5701) Requires the Secretary to submit to the appropriate congressional committees a report on activities carried out under this title and the effectiveness of such activities.

Title VI: Transparency and Program Integrity

Subtitle A: Physician Ownership and Other Transparency

(Sec. 6001, as modified by Sec. 10601) Amends SSA title XVIII (Medicare) to prohibit physician-owned hospitals that do not have a provider agreement by August 1, 2010, to participate in Medicare.

Allows their participation in Medicare under a rural provider and hospital exception to the ownership or investment prohibition if they meet certain requirements addressing conflict of interest, bona fide investments, patient safety issues, and expansion limitations.

(Sec. 6002) Amends SSA title XI to require drug, device, biological and medical supply manufacturers to report to the Secretary transfers of value made to a physician, physician medical practice, a physician group practice, and/or teaching hospital, as well as information on any physician ownership or investment interest in the manufacturer. Provides penalties for noncompliance. Preempts duplicative state or local laws.

(Sec. 6003) Amends SSA title XVIII (Medicare), with respect to the Medicare in-office ancillary exception to the prohibition against physician self-referrals, to require a referring physician to inform the patient in writing that the patient may obtain a specified imaging service from a person other than the referring physician, a physician who is a member of the same group practice as the referring physician, or an individual directly supervised by the physician or by another physician in the group practice. Requires the referring physician also to provide the patient with a written list of suppliers who furnish such services in the area in which the patient resides.

(Sec. 6004) Amends SSA title XI to require prescription drug manufacturers and authorized distributors of record to report to the Secretary specified information pertaining to drug samples.

(Sec. 6005) Amends SSA title XI to require a pharmacy benefit manager (PBM) or a health benefits plan that manages prescription drug coverage under a contract with a Medicare or Exchange health plan to report to the Secretary information regarding the generic dispensing rate, the rebates, discounts, or price concessions negotiated by the PBM, and the payment difference between health plans and PBMs and the PBMs and pharmacies.

Subtitle B: Nursing Home Transparency and Improvement

Part I: Improving Transparency of Information

(Sec. 6101) Amends SSA title XI to require SNFs under Medicare and nursing facilities (NFs) under Medicaid to make available, upon request by the Secretary, the HHS Inspector General, the states, or a state long-term care ombudsman, information on ownership of the SNF or NF, including a description of the facility's governing body and organizational structure, as well as information regarding additional disclosable parties.

(Sec. 6102) Requires SNFs and NFs to operate a compliance and ethics program effective in preventing and detecting criminal, civil, and administrative violations.

Directs the Secretary to establish and implement a quality assurance and performance improvement program for SNFs and NFs, including multi-unit chains of facilities.

(Sec. 6103) Amends SSA title XVIII (Medicare) to require the Secretary to publish on the Nursing Home Compare Medicare website: (1) standardized staffing data; (2) links to state websites regarding state survey and certification programs; (3) the model standardized complaint form; (4) a summary of substantiated complaints; and (5) the number of adjudicated instances of criminal violations by a facility or its employees.

(Sec. 6104) Requires SNFs to report separately expenditures on wages and benefits for direct care staff, breaking out registered nurses, licensed professional nurses, certified nurse assistants, and other medical and therapy staff.

(Sec. 6105) Requires the Secretary to develop a standardized complaint form for use by residents (or a person acting on a resident's behalf) in filing complaints with a state survey and certification agency and a state long-term care ombudsman program. Requires states to establish complaint resolution processes.

(Sec. 6106) Amends SSA title XI to require the Secretary to develop a program for facilities to report direct care staffing information on payroll and other verifiable and auditable data in a uniform format.

(Sec. 6107) Requires the Comptroller General to study and report to Congress on the Five-Star Quality Rating System for nursing homes of CMS.

Part II: Targeting Enforcement

(Sec. 6111) Amends SSA title XVIII (Medicare) to authorize the Secretary to reduce civil monetary penalties by 50% for certain SNFs and NFs that self-report and promptly correct deficiencies within 10 calendar days of imposition of the penalty. Directs the Secretary to issue regulations providing for an informal dispute resolution process after imposition of a penalty, as well as an escrow account for money penalties pending resolution of any appeals.

(Sec. 6112) Directs the Secretary to establish a demonstration project for developing, testing, and implementing a national independent monitor program to oversee interstate and large intrastate chains of SNFs and NFs.

(Sec. 6113) Requires the administrator of a SNF or a NF that is preparing to close to notify in writing residents, legal representatives of residents or other responsible parties, the Secretary, and the state long-term care ombudsman program in advance of the closure by at least 60 days. Requires the notice to include a plan for the transfer and adequate relocation of residents to another facility or alternative setting. Requires the state to ensure a successful relocation of residents.

(Sec. 6114) Requires the Secretary to conduct two SNF- and NF-based demonstration projects to develop best practice models in two areas: (1) one for facilities involved in the "culture change" movement; and (2) one for the use of information technology to improve resident care.

Part III: Improving Staff Training

(Sec. 6121) Requires SNFs and NFs to include dementia management and abuse prevention training as part of pre-employment initial training and, if appropriate, as part of ongoing in-service training for permanent and contract or agency staff.

Subtitle C: Nationwide Program for National and State Background Checks on Direct Patient Access Employees of Long-Term Care Facilities and Providers

(Sec. 6201) Requires the Secretary to establish a nationwide program for national and state background checks on prospective direct patient access employees of long-term care facilities and providers.

Subtitle D: Patient-Centered Outcomes Research

(Sec. 6301, as modified by Sec. 10602) Amends SSA title XI to establish the Patient-Centered Outcomes Research Institute to identify priorities for, and establish, update, and carry out a national comparative outcomes research project agenda. Provides for a peer review process for primary research.

Prohibits the Institute from allowing the subsequent use of data from original research in work-for-hire contracts with individuals, entities, or instrumentalities that have a financial interest in the results, unless approved by the Institute under a data use agreement.

Amends the Public Health Service Act to direct the Office of Communication and Knowledge Transfer at AHRQ to disseminate broadly the research findings published by the Institute and other government-funded research relevant to comparative clinical effective research.

Prohibits the Secretary from using evidence and findings from Institute research to make a determination regarding Medicare coverage unless such use is through an iterative and transparent process which includes public comment and considers the effect on subpopulations.

Amends the Internal Revenue Code to establish in the Treasury the Patient-Centered Outcomes Research Trust Fund. Directs the Secretary to make transfers to that Trust Fund from the Medicare Trust Funds.

Imposes annual fees of $2 times the number of insured lives on each specified health insurance policy and on self-insured health plans.

(Sec. 6302) Terminates the Federal Coordinating Council for Comparative Effectiveness Research upon enactment of this Act.

Subtitle E: Medicare, Medicaid, and CHIP Program Integrity Provisions

(Sec. 6401, as modified by Sec. 10603) Amends SSA title XVIII (Medicare) to require the Secretary to: (1) establish procedures for screening providers and suppliers participating in Medicare, Medicaid, and CHIP; and (2) determine the level of screening according to the risk of fraud, waste, and abuse with respect to each category of provider or supplier.

Requires providers and suppliers applying for enrollment or revalidation of enrollment in Medicare, Medicaid, or CHIP to disclose current or previous affiliations with any provider or supplier that: (1) has uncollected debt; (2) has had its payments suspended; (3) has been excluded from participating in a federal health care program; or (4) has had billing privileges revoked. Authorizes the Secretary to deny enrollment in a program if these affiliations pose an undue risk to it.

Requires providers and suppliers to establish a compliance program containing specified core elements.

Directs the CMS Administrator to establish a process for making available to each state agency with responsibility for administering a state Medicaid plan or a child health plan under SSA title XXI the identity of any provider or supplier under Medicare or CHIP who is terminated.

(Sec. 6402) Requires CMS to include in the integrated data repository claims and payment data from Medicare, Medicaid, CHIP, and health-related programs administered by the Departments of Veterans Affairs (VA) and DOD, the Social Security Administration, and IHS.

Directs the Secretary to enter into data-sharing agreements with the Commissioner of Social Security, the VA and DOD Secretaries, and the IHS Director to help identity fraud, waste, and abuse.

Requires that overpayments be reported and returned within 60 days from the date the overpayment was identified or by the date a corresponding cost report was due, whichever is later.

Directs the Secretary to issue a regulation requiring all Medicare, Medicaid, and CHIP providers to include their National Provider Identifier on enrollment applications.

Authorizes the Secretary to withhold the federal matching payment to states for medical assistance expenditures whenever a state does not report enrollee encounter data in a timely manner to the state's Medicaid Management Information System.

Authorizes the Secretary to exclude providers' and suppliers' participation in any federal health care program for providing false information on any application to enroll or participate.

Subjects to civil monetary penalties excluded individuals who: (1) order or prescribe an item or service; (2) make false statements on applications or contracts to participate in a federal health care program; or (3) know of an overpayment and do not return it. Subjects the latter offense to civil monetary penalties of up to $50,000 or triple the total amount of the claim involved.

Authorizes the Secretary to issue subpoenas and require the attendance and testimony of witnesses and the production of any other evidence that relates to matters under investigation or in question.

Requires the Secretary to take into account the volume of billing for a durable medical equipment (DME) supplier or home health agency when determining the size of the supplier's and agency's surety bond. Authorizes the Secretary to require other providers and suppliers to post a surety bond if the Secretary considers them to be at risk.

Authorizes the Secretary to suspend payments to a provider or supplier pending a fraud investigation.

Appropriates an additional $10 million, adjusted for inflation, to the Health Care Fraud and Abuse Control each of FY2011-FY2020. Applies inflation adjustments as well to Medicare Integrity Program funding.

Requires the Medicaid Integrity Program and Program contractors to provide the Secretary and the HHS Office of Inspector General with performance statistics, including the number and amount of overpayments recovered, the number of fraud referrals, and the return on investment for such activities.

(Sec. 6403) Requires the Secretary to furnish the National Practitioner Data Bank (NPDB) with all information reported to the national health care fraud and abuse data collection program on certain final adverse actions taken against health care providers, suppliers, and practitioners.

Requires the Secretary to establish a process to terminate the Healthcare Integrity and Protection Databank (HIPDB) and ensure that the information formerly collected in it is transferred to the NPDB.

(Sec. 6404) Reduces from three years to one year after the date of service the maximum period for submission of Medicare claims.

(Sec. 6405, as modified by Sec. 10604) Requires DME or home health services to be ordered by an enrolled Medicare eligible professional or physician. Authorizes the Secretary to extend these requirements to other Medicare items and services to reduce fraud, waste, and abuse.

(Sec. 6406) Authorizes the Secretary to disenroll, for up to one year, a Medicare enrolled physician or supplier that fails to maintain and provide access to written orders or requests for payment for DME, certification for home health services, or referrals for other items and services.

Authorizes the Secretary to exclude from participation in any federal health care program any individual or entity ordering, referring for furnishing, or certifying the need for an item or service that fails to provide adequate documentation to verify payment.

(Sec. 6407, as modified by Sec. 10605) Requires a physician, nurse practitioner, clinical nurse specialist, certified nurse-midwife, or physician assistant to have a face-to-face encounter with an individual before issuing a certification for home health services or DME.

Authorizes the Secretary to apply the same face-to-face encounter requirement to other items and services based upon a finding that doing so would reduce the risk of fraud, waste, and abuse. Applies the same requirement, as well, to physicians making certifications for home health services under Medicaid.

(Sec. 6408) Revises civil monetary penalties for making false statements or delaying inspections.

Applies specified enhanced sanctions and civil monetary penalties to MA or Part D plans that: (1) enroll individuals in an MA or Part D plan without their consent; (2) transfer an individual from one plan to another for the purpose of earning a commission; (3) fail to comply with marketing requirements and CMS guidance; or (4) employ or contract with an individual or entity that commits a violation.

(Sec. 6409) Requires the Secretary to establish a self-referral disclosure protocol to enable health care providers and suppliers to disclose actual or potential violations of the physician self-referral law.

Authorizes the Secretary to reduce the amount due and owing for all violations of such law.

(Sec. 6410) Requires the Secretary to: (1) expand the number of areas to be included in round two of the competitive bidding program from 79 to 100 of the largest metropolitan statistical areas; and (2) use competitively bid prices in all areas by 2016.

(Sec. 6411) Requires states to establish contracts with one or more Recovery Audit Contractors (RACs), which shall identify underpayments and overpayments and recoup overpayments made for services provided under state Medicaid plans as well as state plan waivers.

Requires the Secretary to expand the RAC program to Medicare Parts C (Medicare+Choice) and D (Prescription Drug Program).

Subtitle F: Additional Medicaid Program Integrity Provisions

(Sec. 6501) Amends SSA title XIX (Medicaid) to require states to terminate individuals or entities (providers) from their Medicaid programs if they were terminated from Medicare or another state's Medicaid program.

(Sec. 6502) Requires Medicaid agencies to exclude individuals or entities from participating in Medicaid for a specified period of time if the entity or individual owns, controls, or manages an entity that: (1) has failed to repay overpayments during a specified period; (2) is suspended, excluded, or terminated from participation in any Medicaid program; or (3) is affiliated with an individual or entity that has been suspended, excluded, or terminated from Medicaid participation.

(Sec. 6503) Requires state Medicaid plans to require any billing agents, clearinghouses, or other alternate payees that submit claims on behalf of health care providers to register with the state and the Secretary.

(Sec. 6504) Requires states to submit data elements from the state mechanized claims processing and information retrieval system (under the Medicaid Statistical Information System) that the Secretary determines necessary for program integrity, program oversight, and administration.

Requires a Medicaid managed care entity contract to provide for maintenance of sufficient patient encounter data to identify the physician who delivers services to patients (as under current law) at a frequency and level of detail to be specified by the Secretary.

(Sec. 6505) Requires a state Medicaid plan to prohibit the state from making any payments for items or services under a Medicaid state plan or a waiver to any financial institution or entity located outside of the United States.

(Sec. 6506) Extends the period for states to recover overpayments from 60 days to one year after discovery of the overpayment. Declares that, when overpayments due to fraud are pending, state repayments of the federal portion of such overpayments shall not be due until 30 days after the date of the final administrative or judicial judgment on the matter.

(Sec. 6507) Requires state mechanized Medicaid claims processing and information retrieval systems to incorporate methodologies compatible with Medicare's National Correct Coding Initiative.

Subtitle G: Additional Program Integrity Provisions

(Sec. 6601) Amends the Employee Retirement Income Security Act of 1974 (ERISA) to prohibit employees and agents of multiple employer welfare arrangements (MEWAs), subject to criminal penalties, from making false statements in marketing materials regarding an employee welfare benefit plan's financial solvency, benefits, or regulatory status.

(Sec. 6603) Amends the Public Health Service Act to direct the Secretary to request NAIC to develop a model uniform report form for a private health insurance issuer seeking to refer suspected fraud and abuse to state insurance departments or other responsible state agencies for investigation.

(Sec. 6604) Amends ERISA to direct the Secretary of Labor to adopt regulatory standards and/or issue orders to subject MEWAs to state law relating to fraud and abuse.

(Sec. 6605) Authorizes the Secretary of Labor to: (1) issue cease-and-desist orders to shut down temporarily the operations of MEWAs conducting fraudulent activities or posing a serious threat to the public, until hearings can be completed; and (2) seize a plan's assets if it appears that the plan is in a financially hazardous condition.

(Sec. 6606) Directs the Secretary of Labor to require MEWAs which are not group health plans to register with the Department of Labor before operating in a state.

(Sec. 6607) Authorizes the Secretary of Labor to promulgate a regulation providing an evidentiary privilege that allows confidential communication among specified federal and state officials relating to investigation of fraud and abuse.

Subtitle H: Elder Justice Act

Elder Justice Act of 2009—(Sec. 6702) Amends SSA title XX (Block Grants to States for Social Services) with respect to elder abuse, neglect, and exploitation and their prevention. Requires the HHS Secretary to award grants and carry out activities that provide: (1) greater protection to those individuals seeking care in facilities that provide long-term care services and supports; and (2) greater incentives for individuals to train and seek employment at such facilities.

Requires facility owners, operators, and certain employees to report suspected crimes committed at a facility.

Requires facility owners or operators also to: (1) submit to the Secretary and to the state written notification of an impending closure of a facility within 60 days before the closure; and (2) include a plan for transfer and adequate relocation of all residents.

Establishes an Elder Justice Coordinating Council.

Subtitle I: Sense of the Senate Regarding Medical Malpractice

(Sec. 6801) Expresses the sense of the Senate that: (1) health reform presents an opportunity to address issues related to medical malpractice and medical liability insurance; (2) states should be encouraged to develop and test alternative models to the existing civil litigation system; and (3) Congress should consider state demonstration projects to evaluate such alternatives.

Title VII: Improving Access to Innovative Medical Therapies

Subtitle A: Biologics Price Competition and Innovation

Biologics Price Competition and Innovation Act of 2009—(Sec. 7002) Amends the Public Health Service Act to allow a person to submit an application for licensure of a biological product based on its similarity to a licensed biological product (the reference product). Requires the Secretary to license the biological product if it is biosimilar to or interchangeable with the reference product.

Prohibits the Secretary from determining that a second or subsequent biological product is interchangeable with a reference product for any condition of use for specified periods based on the marketing of, and the presence or status of litigation involving, the first biosimilar biological product deemed interchangeable with the same reference product.

Prohibits the Secretary from making approval of an application under this Act effective until 12 years after the date on which the reference product was first licensed.

Subtitle B: More Affordable Medicine for Children and Underserved Communities

(Sec. 7101) Expands the 340B drug discount program (a program limiting the cost of covered outpatient drugs to certain federal grantees) to allow participation as a covered entity by certain: (1) children's hospitals; (2) freestanding cancer hospitals; (3) critical access hospitals; (4) rural referral centers; and (5) sole community hospitals. Expands the program to include drugs used in connection with an inpatient or outpatient service by enrolled hospitals (currently, only outpatient drugs are covered under the program).

Requires the Secretary to establish reasonable exceptions to the prohibition on enrolled hospitals obtaining covered outpatient drugs through a group purchasing organization or other group purchasing arrangement, including for drugs unavailable through the program and to facilitate generic substitution when a generic covered drug is available at a lower price. Allows such hospitals to purchase covered drugs for inpatients through any such arrangement.

Requires a hospital enrolled in the 340B drug discount program to issue a credit to a state Medicaid program for inpatient covered drugs provided to Medicaid recipients.

(Sec. 7102) Requires the Secretary to: (1) provide for improvements in compliance by manufacturers and covered entities with the requirements of the 340B drug discount program; and (2) establish and implement an administrative process for resolving claims by covered entities and manufacturers of violations of such requirements.

Requires manufacturers to offer each covered entity covered drugs for purchase at or below the applicable ceiling price if such a drug is made available to any other purchaser at any price.

(Sec. 7103) Requires the Comptroller General to report to Congress on whether those individuals served by the covered entities under the 340B drug discount program are receiving optimal health care services.

Title VIII: Class Act

Community Living Assistance Services and Supports Act or the CLASS Act—(Sec. 8002, as modified by Sec. 10801) Establishes a national, voluntary insurance program for purchasing community living assistance services and supports (CLASS program) under which: (1) all employees are automatically enrolled, but are allowed to waive enrollment; (2) payroll deductions pay monthly premiums; and (3) benefits under a CLASS Independence Benefit Plan provide individuals with functional limitations with tools that will allow them to maintain their personal and financial independence and live in the community.

Title IX: Revenue Provisions

Subtitle A: Revenue Offset Provisions

(Sec. 9001, as modified by section 10901) Amends the Internal Revenue Code to impose an excise tax of 40% of the excess benefit from certain high cost employer-sponsored health coverage. Deems any amount which exceeds payment of $8,500 for an employee self-only coverage plan and $23,000 for employees with other than self-only coverage (family plans) as an excess benefit. Increases such amounts for certain retirees and employees who are engaged in high-risk professions (e.g., law enforcement officers, emergency medical first responders, or longshore workers). Imposes a penalty on employers and coverage providers for failure to calculate the proper amount of an excess benefit.

(Sec. 9002) Requires employers to include in the W-2 form of each employee the aggregate cost of applicable employer-sponsored group health coverage that is excludable from the employee's gross income (excluding the value of contributions to flexible spending arrangements).

(Sec. 9003) Restricts payments from health savings accounts, medical savings accounts, and health flexible spending arrangements for medications to prescription drugs or insulin.

(Sec. 9004) Increases to 20% the penalty for distributions from a health savings account or Archer medical savings account not used for qualified medical expenses.

(Sec. 9005, as modified by section 10902) Limits annual salary reduction contributions by an employee to a health flexible spending arrangement under a cafeteria plan to $2,500. Allows an annual inflation adjustment to such amount after 2011.

(Sec. 9006) Applies to corporations reporting requirements for payments of $600 or more to persons engaged in a trade or business.

(Sec. 9007, as modified by section 10903) Requires tax-exempt charitable hospitals to: (1) conduct a community health needs assessment every two years; (2) adopt a written financial assistance policy for patients who require financial assistance for hospital care; and (3) refrain from taking extraordinary collection actions against a patient until the hospital has made reasonable efforts to determine whether the patient is eligible for financial assistance. Imposes a penalty tax on hospitals that fail to comply with the requirements of this Act.

Requires the Secretary of the Treasury to report to Congress on information with respect to private tax-exempt, taxable, and government-owned hospitals regarding levels of charity care provided, bad debt expenses, unreimbursed costs, and costs for community benefit activities.

(Sec. 9008) Imposes an annual fee on the branded prescription drug sales exceeding $5 million of manufacturers and importers of such drugs beginning in 2010. Requires the HHS, VA, and DOD Secretaries to report to the Secretary of the Treasury on the total branded prescription drug sales within government programs within their departments.

(Sec. 9009, as modified by section 10904) Imposes an annual fee on the gross sales receipts exceeding $5 million of manufacturers and importers of certain medical devices beginning in 2011.

(Sec. 9010, as modified by section 10905) Imposes on any entity that provides health insurance for any United States health risk an annual fee beginning in 2011. Defines "United States health risk" as the health risk of an individual who is a U.S. citizen or resident or is located in the United States with respect to the period the individual is so located. Exempts entities whose net premiums written are not more than $25 million. Requires all entities subject to such fee to report to the Secretary of the Treasury on their net written premiums and imposes a penalty for failure to report.

(Sec. 9011) Requires the VA Secretary to study and report to Congress by December 31, 2012, on the effect of fees assessed by this Act on the cost of medical care provided to veterans and on veterans' access to medical devices and branded prescription drugs.

(Sec. 9012) Eliminates the tax deduction for expenses for determining the subsidy for employers who maintain prescription drug plans for Medicare Part D eligible retirees.

(Sec. 9013) Increases the adjusted gross income threshold for claiming the itemized deduction for medical expenses from 7.5% to 10% beginning after 2012. Retains the 7.5% threshold through 2016 for individual taxpayers who have attained age 65 before the close of an applicable taxable year.

(Sec. 9014) Imposes a limitation after December 31, 2012, of $500,000 on the deductibility of remuneration paid to officers, directors, employees, and service providers of health insurance issuers who derive at least 25% of their gross premiums from providing health insurance coverage that meets the minimum essential coverage requirements established by this Act.

(Sec. 9015, as modified by section 10906) Increases after December 31, 2012, the hospital insurance tax rate by .9% for individual taxpayers earning over $200,000 ($250,000 for married couples filing joint tax returns).

(Sec. 9016) Requires Blue Cross or Blue Shield organizations or other nonprofit organizations that provide health insurance to reimburse at least 85% of the cost of clinical services provided to their enrollees to be eligible for special tax benefits currently provided to such organizations.

Subtitle B: Other Provisions

(Sec. 9021) Excludes from gross income the value of certain health benefits provided to members of Indian tribes, including: (1) health services or benefits provided or purchased by IHS; (2) medical care provided by an Indian tribe or tribal organization to a member of an Indian tribe; (3) accident or health plan coverage provided by an Indian tribe or tribal organization for medical care to a member of an Indian tribe and dependents; and (4) any other medical care provided by an Indian tribe that supplements, replaces, or substitutes for federal programs.

(Sec. 9022) Establishes a new employee benefit cafeteria plan to be known as a Simple Cafeteria Plan, defined as a plan that: (1) is established and maintained by an employer with an average of 100 or fewer employees during a two-year period; (2) requires employers to make contributions or match employee contributions to the plan; and (3) requires participating employees to have at least 1,000 hours of service for the preceding plan year; and (4) allows such employees to elect any benefit available under the plan.

(Sec. 9023) Allows a 50% tax credit for investment in any qualifying therapeutic discovery project, defined as a project that is designed to: (1) treat or prevent diseases by conducting pre-clinical activities, clinical trials, and clinical studies, or carrying out research projects to approve new drugs or other biologic products; (2) diagnose diseases or conditions to determine molecular factors related to diseases or conditions; or (3) develop a product, process, or technology to further the delivery or administration of therapeutics. Directs the Secretary of the Treasury to award grants for 50% of the investment in 2009 or 2010 in such a project, in lieu of the tax credit.

Title X: Strengthening Quality, Affordable Health Care for All Americans

Subtitle A: Provisions Relating to Title I

(Sec. 10101) Revises provisions of or related to Subtitles A, B, and C of Title I of this Act (as reflected in the summary of those provisions).

(Sec. 10104) Revises provisions of or related to Subtitle D of Title I of this Act (as reflected in the summary of those provisions). Makes changes to the False Claims Act related to the public disclosure bar on filing civil claims.

(Sec. 10105) Revises provisions of or related to Subtitles E, F, and G of Title I of this Act (as reflected in the summary of those provisions).

(Sec. 10108) Requires an offering employer to provide free choice vouchers to each qualified employee. Defines "offering employer" to mean any employer who offers minimum essential coverage to its employees consisting of coverage through an eligible employer-sponsored plan and who pays any portion of the costs of such plan. Defines "qualified employee" as an employee whose required contribution for such coverage and household income fall within a specified range. Requires: (1) a Health Insurance Exchange to credit the amount of any free choice voucher to the monthly premium of any qualified health plan in which the employee is enrolled; and (2) the offering employer to pay any amounts so credited to the Exchange. Excludes the amount of any free choice voucher from the gross income of the employee. Permits a deduction by employers for such costs.

(Sec. 10109) Amends the SSA to require the HHS Secretary to seek input to determine if there could be greater uniformity in financial and administrative health care activities and items.

Requires the Secretary to: (1) task the ICD-9-CM Coordination and Maintenance Committee to convene a meeting to receive input regarding and recommend revisions to the crosswalk between the Ninth and Tenth Revisions of the International Classification of Diseases; and (2) make appropriate revisions to such crosswalk.

Subtitle B: Provisions Relating to Title II

Part I: Medicaid and CHIP

(Sec. 10201) Revises provisions of Subtitles A through L of Title II of this Act (as reflected in the summary of those provisions).

Amends SSA title XIX (Medicaid) to set the FMAP for the state of Nebraska, with respect to all or any portion of a fiscal year that begins on or after January 1, 2017, at 100% (thus requiring the federal government to pay 100% of the cost of covering newly-eligible individuals in Nebraska).

Directs the Comptroller General to study and report to Congress on whether the development, recognition, or implementation of any specified health care quality guideline or other standards would result in the establishment of a new cause of action or claim.

(Sec. 10202) Creates a State Balancing Incentive Payments Program to increase the FMAP for states which offer home and community-based services as a long-term care alternative to nursing homes.

(Sec. 10203) Amends SSA title XXI (CHIP) to make appropriations for CHIP through FY2015 and revise other CHIP-related requirements.

Part II: Support for Pregnant and Parenting Teens and Women

(Sec. 10212) Requires the Secretary to establish a Pregnancy Assistance Fund for grants to states to assist pregnant and parenting teens and women.

(Sec. 10214) Authorizes appropriations for FY2010-FY2019.

Part III: Indian Health Care Improvement

(Sec. 10221) Enacts into law the Indian Health Care Improvement Reauthorization and Extension Act of 2009 (S. 1790) as reported by the Senate Committee on Indian Affairs in December 2009 and with the following changes.

Amends the Indian Health Care Improvement Act, as amended by the Indian Health Care Improvement Reauthorization and Extension Act of 2009, to make an exception to the requirement that a national Community Health Aide Program exclude dental health aide therapist services. Declares that the exclusion of dental health aide therapist services from services covered under the national program shall not apply where an Indian tribe or tribal organization, located in a state (other than Alaska) in which state law authorizes the use of dental health aide therapist services or midlevel dental health provider services, elects to supply such services in accordance with state law.

Subtitle C: Provisions Relating to Title III

(Sec. 10301) Revises provisions of Subtitles A through G of Title III of this Act (as reflected in the summary of those provisions).

(Sec. 10323) Amends SSA title XVIII (Medicare) to deem eligible for Medicare coverage certain individuals exposed to environmental health hazards.

Directs the Secretary to establish a pilot program for care of certain individuals residing in emergency declaration areas.

Amends SSA title XX (Block Grants to States for Social Services) to direct the Secretary to establish a program for early detection of certain medical conditions related to environmental health hazards. Makes appropriations for FY2012-FY2019.

(Sec. 10324) Establishes floors: (1) on the area wage index for hospitals in frontier states; (2) on the area wage adjustment factor for hospital outpatient department services in frontier states; and (3) for the practice expense index for services furnished in frontier states.

(Sec. 10325) Revises the SNF prospective payment system to delay specified changes until FY2011.

(Sec. 10326) Directs the Secretary to conduct separate pilot programs, for specified kinds of hospitals and hospice programs, to test the implementation of a value-based purchasing program for payments to the provider.

(Sec. 10327) Authorizes an additional incentive payment under the physician quality reporting system in 2011 through 2014 to eligible professionals who report quality measures to CMS via a qualified Maintenance of Certification program. Eliminates the MedicareAdvantage Regional Plan Stabilization Fund.

(Sec. 10328) Requires Medicare Part D prescription drug plans to include a comprehensive review of medications as part of their medication therapy management programs. Requires automatic quarterly enrollment of qualified beneficiaries, with an allowance for them to opt out.

(Sec. 10329) Requires the Secretary to develop a methodology to measure health plan value.

(Sec. 10330) Directs the Secretary to develop a plan to modernize CMS computer and data systems.

(Sec. 10331) Requires the Secretary to: (1) develop a Physician Compare website with information on physicians enrolled in the Medicare program and other eligible professionals who participate in the Physician Quality Reporting Initiative; and (2) implement a plan to make information on physician performance public through Physician Compare, particularly quality and patient experience measures.

Authorizes the Secretary to provide financial incentives to Medicare beneficiaries furnished services by high quality physicians.

(Sec. 10332) Directs the Secretary to make available to qualified entities standardized extracts of Medicare claims data for the evaluation of the performance of service providers and suppliers.

(Sec. 10333) Amends the Public Health Service Act to authorize the Secretary to award grants to eligible entities to support community-based collaborative care networks for low-income populations.

(Sec. 10334) Transfers the Office of Minority Health to the Office of the Secretary. Authorizes appropriations for FY2011-FY2016.

Establishes individual offices of minority health within HHS.

Redesignates the National Center on Minority Health and Health Disparities in NIH as the National Institute on Minority Health and Health Disparities.

(Sec. 10336) Directs the Comptroller General to study and report to Congress on the impact on Medicare beneficiary access to high-quality dialysis services including specified oral drugs furnished to them for the treatment of end stage renal disease in the related bundled prospective payment system.

Subtitle D: Provisions Relating to Title IV

(Sec. 10401) Revises provisions of or related to Subtitles A, B, C, D, and E of Title IV of this Act (as reflected in the summary of those provisions).

(Sec. 10407) Catalyst to Better Diabetes Care Act of 2009—Requires the Secretary to prepare biennially a national diabetes report card and, to the extent possible, one for each state.

Requires the Secretary, acting through the Director of CDC, to: (1) promote the education and training of physicians on the importance of birth and death certificate data and on how to properly complete these documents; (2) encourage state adoption of the latest standard revisions of birth and death certificates; and (3) work with states to reengineer their vital statistics systems in order to provide cost-effective, timely, and accurate vital systems data. Allows the Secretary to promote improvements to the collection of diabetes mortality data.

Directs the Secretary to conduct a study of the impact of diabetes on the practice of medicine in the United States and the level of diabetes medical education that should be required prior to licensure, board certification, and board recertification.

(Sec. 10408) Requires the Secretary to award grants to eligible employers to provide their employees with access to comprehensive workplace wellness programs.

(Sec. 10409) Cures Acceleration Network Act of 2009—Amends the Public Health Service Act to require the Secretary, acting through the Director of NIH, to implement the Cures Acceleration Network under which grants and contracts will be awarded to accelerate the development of high need cures. Defines "high need cure" as a drug, biological product, or device: (1) that is a priority to diagnose, mitigate, prevent, or treat harm from any disease or condition; and (2) for which the incentives of the commercial market are unlikely to result in its adequate or timely development. Establishes a Cures Acceleration Network Review Board.

(Sec. 10410) Establishing a Network of Health-Advancing National Centers of Excellence for Depression Act of 2009 or the ENHANCED Act of 2009—Requires the Secretary, acting through the Administrator of the Substance Abuse and Mental Health Services Administration, to: (1) award grants to establish national centers of excellence for depression; and (2) designate one such center as a coordinating center. Requires the coordinating center to establish and maintain a national, publicly available database to improve prevention programs, evidence-based interventions, and disease management programs for depressive disorders using data collected from the national centers.

(Sec. 10411) Congenital Heart Futures Act—Authorizes the Secretary, acting through the Director of CDC, to: (1) enhance and expand infrastructure to track the epidemiology of congenital heart disease and to organize such information into the National Congenital Heart Disease Surveillance System; or (2) award a grant to an eligible entity to undertake such activities.

Authorizes the Director of the National Heart, Lung, and Blood Institute to expand, intensify, and coordinate research and related Institute activities on congenital heart disease.

(Sec. 10412) Reauthorizes appropriations for grants for public access defibrillation programs. Requires an information clearinghouse to increase public access to defibrillation in schools established under such programs to be administered by an organization that has substantial expertise in pediatric education, pediatric medicine, and electrophysiology and sudden death.

(Sec. 10413) Young Women's Breast Health Education and Awareness Requires Learning Young Act of 2009 or the EARLY Act—Requires the Secretary, acting through the Director of CDC, to conduct: (1) a national education campaign to increase awareness of young women's knowledge regarding breast health and breast cancer; (2) an education campaign among physicians and other health care professionals to increase awareness of breast health of young women; and (3) prevention research on breast cancer in younger women.

Requires the Secretary, acting through the Director of NIH, to conduct research to develop and validate new screening tests and methods for prevention and early detection of breast cancer in young women.

Directs the Secretary to award grants for the provision of health information to young women diagnosed with breast cancer and pre-neoplastic breast diseases.

Subtitle E: Provisions Relating to Title V

(Sec. 10501) Revises provisions of or related to Title V of this Act (as reflected in the summary of those provisions).

Requires the Secretary, acting through the Director of CDC, to establish a national diabetes prevention program targeted at adults at high risk for diabetes.

Directs the Secretary to develop a Medicare prospective payment system for payment for services furnished by federally qualified health centers.

Requires the Secretary, acting through the Administrator of the HRSA, to establish a grant program to assist accredited schools of allopathic or osteopathic medicine in: (1) recruiting students most likely to practice medicine in underserved rural communities; (2) providing rural-focused training and experience; and (3) increasing the number of recent allopathic and osteopathic medical school graduates who practice in underserved rural communities.

Directs the Secretary, acting through the Administrator of HRSA, to award grants or enter into contracts with eligible entities to provide training to graduate medical residents in preventive medicine specialties.

Reauthorizes appropriations for public health workforce activities.

Revises provisions related to fulfillment of service obligations under the National Health Service Corps related to half-time clinical practice and teaching.

(Sec. 10502) Authorizes appropriations to HHS for debt service on, or direct construction or renovation of, a health care facility that provides research, inpatient tertiary care, or outpatient clinical services and that meets certain requirements, including that it is critical for the provision of greater access to health care within the state.

(Sec. 10503) Establishes a Community Health Center Fund to provide for expanded and sustained national investment in community health centers. Authorizes appropriations to such Fund.

(Sec. 10504) Requires the Secretary, acting through the Administrator of HRSA, to establish a demonstration project to provide access to comprehensive health care services to the uninsured at reduced fees.

Subtitle F: Provisions Relating to Title VI

(Sec. 10601) Revises provisions of Subtitles A through E of Title VI of this Act (as reflected in the summary of those provisions).

(Sec. 10606) Directs the U.S. Sentencing Commission to amend the Federal Sentencing Guidelines to provide two-level, three-level, and four-level increases in the offense level for any defendant convicted of a federal health care offense relating to a government health care program of a loss between $1 million and $7 million, between $7 million and $20 million, and at least $20 million, respectively.

Provides that a person need not have actual knowledge of the prohibition against health care fraud nor specific intent to violate it in order to commit health care fraud.

Expands the scope of violations constituting a federal health care offense.

Amends the Civil Rights of Institutionalized Persons Act to authorize the Attorney General to require access to an institution by subpoena to investigate conditions depriving residents of specified constitutional or federal rights.

(Sec. 10607) Authorizes the Secretary to award demonstration grants to states for the development, implementation, and evaluation of alternatives to current tort litigation for resolving disputes over injuries allegedly caused by health care providers or health care organizations.

(Sec. 10608) Amends the Public Health Service Act to extend medical malpractice coverage to free clinics by deeming their officers, employees, board members, and contractors to be employees of the Public Health Service.

(Sec. 10609) Amends the Federal Food, Drug, and Cosmetic Act to set forth circumstances under which a generic drug may be approved with a label different from the listed drug.

Subtitle G: Provisions Relating to Title VIII

(Sec. 10801) Revises provisions of or related to Title VIII of this Act (as reflected in the summary of those provisions).

Subtitle H: Provisions Relating to Title IX

(Sec. 10901) Revises provisions of or related to Title IX of this Act (as reflected in the summary of those provisions).

(Sec. 10907) Amends the Internal Revenue Code to impose a 10% excise tax on any amount paid for indoor tanning services on or after July 1, 2010. Exempts phototherapy services performed by a licensed medical professional from the definition of "indoor tanning services."

(Sec. 10908) Excludes from gross income any payments under the National Health Service Corps Loan Repayment Program and any other state loan repayment or forgiveness programs intended to increase the availability of health care services in underserved or health professional shortage areas.

(Sec. 10909) Increases from $10,000 to $13,170 the dollar limitation on: (1) the tax credit for adoption expenses; and (2) the tax exclusion for employer-provided adoption assistance. Allows an inflation adjustment to such limitation after 2010. Makes such credit refundable. Extends through 2011 the general terminating date of the Economic Growth and Tax Relief Reconciliation Act of 2001 with respect to such credit and exclusion.

Health Care and Education Reconciliation Act of 2010 (H.R.4872)

Sponsor: Rep John M. Spratt Jr. [SC-5] (introduced 3/17/2010)   Cosponsors (None)
Became Public Law No: 111-152
Note: The bill makes a number of health-related financing and revenue changes to the Patient Protection and Affordable Care Act enacted by H.R.3590 and modifies higher education assistance provisions.

Title I: Coverage, Medicare, Medicaid, and Revenues

Subtitle A: Coverage

(Sec. 1001) Amends Internal Revenue Code provisions added by the Patient Protection and Affordable Care Act (PPACA) to revise the formula for calculating the refundable tax credit for premium assistance for coverage under a qualified health plan by establishing a sliding scale from the initial to the final premium percentage for individuals and families with household incomes up to 400% of the federal poverty line. Requires adjustments, after 2014 and after 2018, of the initial and final premium percentages to reflect the excess (if any) of the rate of premium growth over the rate of growth of income and the consumer price index.

Reduces from 9.8% to 9.5% of a taxpayer's household income the maximum amount an employee's required contribution to an employer-sponsored plan may be for such employee to be treated as eligible for employer-sponsored minimum essential coverage.

Increases the percentage of employer cost sharing for the out-of-pocket expenses of individuals with household incomes between 100% and 400% of the federal poverty line.

(Sec. 1002) Revises the provisions setting forth penalties to be imposed on individuals who decline to purchase health care coverage by: (1) lowering the maximum penalty amount from $495 to $325 in 2015 and from $750 to $695 in 2016; and (2) increasing the penalty rates based on taxpayer household income for taxable years beginning in 2014 and 2015 and for taxable years beginning after 2015.

(Sec. 1003) Revises the provisions setting forth penalties to be imposed on employers with 50 or more employees who decline to offer employees health care coverage to allow an exemption for the first 30 employees (including part-time employees) when calculating the penalty. Increases the applicable penalty amount per employee to $2,000. Eliminates the assessment on large employers with extended waiting periods for enrollment in employer-sponsored plans.

(Sec. 1004) Modifies the definition of "modified adjusted gross income" for purposes of the tax credit for premium assistance and the individual responsibility requirement for purchasing health care coverage.

Extends the exclusion from gross income for employer-provided health care coverage to adult children up to age 26.

Requires Exchanges that offer health care plans to provide the Secretary of the Treasury and taxpayers with specified information, including information about the level of coverage, the total premium for coverage, and the aggregate amount of any advance payment of the premium assistance tax credit.

Amends title XIX (Medicaid) of the Social Security Act to allow a disregard of 5% of modified adjusted gross income for purposes of determining eligibility for medical assistance.

(Sec. 1005) Establishes a Health Insurance Reform Implementation Fund within the Department of Health and Human Services (HHS) and makes appropriations to the Fund for the administrative costs of carrying out PPACA and this Act.

Subtitle B: Medicare

(Sec. 1101) Amends Part D (Voluntary Prescription Drug Benefit Program) of title XVIII (Medicare) of the Social Security Act (SSA) to direct the Secretary of HHS to provide a one-time $250 rebate in 2010 to all Medicare Part D enrollees who enter the Medicare Part D coverage gap (also known as the Medicare donut hole, the difference between the standard initial coverage limit and the catastrophic or out-of-pocket coverage threshold for which the Medicare beneficiary is financially responsible).

Amends PPACA to: (1) delay until January 1, 2011, the deadline for establishment of a Medicare coverage gap discount program, as well as the effective date of the requirement that a Part D drug manufacturer participate in it; and (2) repeal the increase by $500 in the 2010 standard initial coverage limit (thus restoring the provisions in effect before enactment of PPACA).

Amends SSA title XVIII, as amended by PPACA, to reduce the coinsurance percentage for covered brand-name and generic drugs to 25% by 2020 (thus closing the donut hole with 75% discounts).

Revises the growth rate of the out-of-pocket cost threshold.

(Sec. 1102) Amends PPACA to repeal: (1) certain provisions concerning MedicareAdvantage (MA) payments, benchmarks, and capitation rates; and (2) a requirement that the Secretary analyze the differences in coding patterns between MA and the original Medicare fee-for-service programs, and incorporate the results into risk scores for 2014 and subsequent years.

Amends SSA title XVIII to freeze MA payments in 2011. Reduces MA benchmarks relative to current levels, varying them from 95% of Medicare spending in high-cost areas to 115% of Medicare spending in low-cost areas. Creates an incentive system to increase payments to high-quality plans by at least 5%. Extends the authority of the Centers for Medicare & Medicaid Services to adjust MA risk scores for observed differences in coding patterns relative to fee-for-service.

Repeals the Comparative Cost Adjustment Program under the Medicare Prescription Drug, Improvement, and Modernization Act of 2003.

(Sec. 1103) Requires MA plans whose medical loss ratios are not at least .85 to remit to the Secretary an amount equal to a specified percentage of plan revenue. Requires the Secretary to: (1) prohibit enrollment in such a plan of new enrollees for three consecutive contract years; and (2) terminate the Medicare+Choice contract if the plan fails to have a .85 medical loss ratio for five consecutive contract years.

(Sec. 1104) Amends SSA title XVIII (Medicare), as amended by PPACA, with respect to specified reductions to Medicare disproportionate share hospital (DSH) payments for FY2015 and ensuing fiscal years, especially to subsection (d) hospitals, to reflect lower uncompensated care costs relative to increases in the number of insured. (Generally, a subsection [d] hospital is an acute care hospital, particularly one that receives payments under Medicare's inpatient prospective payment system [IPPS] when providing covered inpatient services to eligible beneficiaries.)

Advances the beginning of such reductions from FY2015 to FY2014. Revises the reduction formula to lower the reduction scheduled to occur over ten years.

(Sec. 1105) Revises the hospital market basket reduction applicable to payments to inpatient hospitals, long-term care hospitals, inpatient rehabilitation facilities, psychiatric hospitals, and out-patient hospitals.

(Sec. 1106) Postpones from August 1, 2010, to December 31, 2010, the date by which physician-owned hospitals must have a provider agreement in order to participate in Medicare under a rural provider and hospital exception to the physician-ownership or -investment prohibition if they also meet certain requirements addressing conflicts of interest, bona fide investments, patient safety issues, and expansion limitations.

Modifies the expansion limitation imposed on such a rural hospital under which the number of operating rooms, procedure rooms, and beds for which the hospital is licensed at any time on or after the enactment of PPACA is no greater than the number of such rooms and beds for which the hospital is licensed as of such date. Allows an exception to the expansion limitation for a high Medicaid hospital that treats the highest percentage of Medicaid patients in their county (and is not the sole hospital in the county).

(Sec. 1107) Revises the special rule in the physician fee schedule for imaging services, in particular the PPACA adjustment in the practice expense relative value units, with respect to advanced diagnostic imaging services to reflect a higher presumed utilization rate. Replaces the multiyear phase-in of the assumed utilization rate from 50% to 75% with a flat 75% rate for 2011 and subsequent years.

(Sec. 1108) Modifies the employee wage and rent portions of the practice expense geographic index adjustment for 2010 and subsequent years. Requires such portions to reflect 1/2 (instead of 3/4) of the difference between the relative costs of employee wages and rents in each of the different fee schedule areas and the national average of such employee wages and rents.

(Sec. 1109) Directs the Secretary to provide for a specified payment for FY2011 and FY2012 to qualifying subsection (d) hospitals located in a county that ranks, based upon age, sex, and race adjusted spending per enrollee for Medicare Parts A and B benefits, within the lowest quartile of such counties in the United States.

Subtitle C: Medicaid

(Sec. 1201) Amends SSA title XIX (Medicaid), as amended by PPACA, to repeal the permanent 100% federal matching rate (federal medical assistance percentage [FMAP]) for Nebraska for the Medicaid costs of newly eligible mandatory individuals (expansion populations). Provides federal Medicaid matching payments for the costs of services to expansion populations at the following rates in all states: (1) 100% in 2014, 2015, and 2016; (2) 95% in 2017; (3) 94% in 2018; (4) 93% in 2019; and (5) 90% thereafter.

Reduces, in the case of expansion states, the state share of the costs of covering nonpregnant childless adults by 50% in 2014, 60% in 2015, 70% in 2016, 80% in 2017, 90% in 2018.

(Sec. 1202) Requires that Medicaid payment rates to primary care physicians (family medicine, general internal medicine, or pediatric medicine) for furnishing primary care services in 2013 and 2014 be at least 100% of Medicare payment rates under both fee-for-service plans and managed-care plans.

Requires a 100% FMAP for the costs to states of meeting this requirement.

(Sec. 1203) Lowers the reduction in federal Medicaid DSH payments and advances the reductions to begin in FY2014.

Directs the Secretary to develop a methodology for reducing federal DSH allotments to all states in order to achieve the mandated reductions.

Extends through FY2013 the federal DSH allotment for a state that has a $0 allotment after FY2011.

(Sec. 1204) Authorizes Puerto Rico, Virgin Islands, Guam, American Samoa, and the Northern Mariana Islands to elect to operate a Health Benefits Exchange. Increases federal Medicaid payments to such territories. Raises the caps on federal Medicaid funding for each of the territories.

(Sec. 1205) Postpones from October 1, 2010, until October 1, 2011, the effective date of the Community First Choice option established for state Medicaid programs to offer home and community-based attendant services and supports to Medicaid beneficiaries with disabilities who would otherwise require care in a hospital, nursing facility, intermediate care facility for the mentally retarded, or an institution for mental diseases.

(Sec. 1206) Revises the definition of a new formulation of an existing drug, for purposes of applying the additional rebate, to specify a line extension of a single source drug or an innovator multiple source drug that is an oral solid dosage form of the drug.

Subtitle D: Reducing Fraud, Waste, and Abuse

(Sec. 1301) Revises the meaning of a community mental health center that provides Medicare partial hospitalization services as a distinct and organized intensive ambulatory treatment service offering less than 24-hour-daily care. Establishes new requirements for such community mental health centers. Requires such a center to provide: (1) daily care other than in an individual's home or in an inpatient or residential setting; and (2) at least 40% of its services to individuals who are not eligible for Medicare benefits.

(Sec. 1302) Repeals Medicare prepayment medical review limitations to facilitate additional reviews designed to reduce fraud and abuse.

(Sec. 1303) Makes additional appropriations to the Health Care Fraud and Abuse Control Account of the Federal Hospital Insurance Trust Fund for FY2011-FY2016.

Makes additional appropriations to the Medicare Integrity Program for FY2010 and each subsequent year, indexed for inflation.

(Sec. 1305) Revises requirements for the enrollment process for Medicare service providers and suppliers. Requires the Secretary to: (1) withhold payment for a 90-day period after submission of a claim; and (2) conduct enhanced oversight in cases where the Secretary identifies a significant risk of fraud among newly enrolling durable medical equipment (DME) suppliers in a particular category or geographical area.

Subtitle E: Provisions Relating to Revenue

(Sec. 1401) Amends the Internal Revenue Code to delay until 2018 the excise tax on high cost employer-sponsored health coverage plans. Increases the dollar thresholds for such tax to $10,200 for self-only coverage and $27,500 for other than self-only coverage (family plans). Increases such threshold amounts for retirees and employees in high risk professions. Excludes separate dental and vision plans from such tax. Allows employers to reduce the cost of plan coverage when applying such tax based upon the age and gender characteristics of all plan employees.

(Sec. 1402) Includes net investment income in the Medicare taxable base and imposes a 3.8% tax on such income, beginning in 2013. Excludes from such tax the net investment income of taxpayers with adjusted gross incomes of less than $200,000 ($250,000 for joint returns). Defines "net investment income" to include interest, dividends, annuities, royalties, rents, passive income, and net gain from the disposition of nonbusiness property.

(Sec. 1403) Amends PPACA to delay until 2013 the $2,500 limitation on annual salary reduction contributions by an employee to a health flexible spending arrangement under a cafeteria plan. Delays until 2014 the annual inflation adjustment to such limitation amount.

(Sec. 1404) Delays until 2011 the fee on sales of branded prescription drugs. Sets forth a schedule of applicable amounts for 2011 through 2018 upon which such fee is based.

(Sec. 1405) Imposes a tax on sales after 2012 of any taxable medical device by the manufacturer, producer, or importer equal to 2.3% of the price for which such device is sold. Defines "taxable medical device" as any device intended for humans, except eyeglasses, contact lenses, hearing aids, and any other medical device generally purchased by the general public at retail. Repeals the excise tax on medical devices enacted by PPACA.

(Sec. 1406) Delays until 2014 the annual fee on the net premium income of health insurance providers. Allows a reduced fee for tax-exempt insurance providers. Sets forth a schedule of applicable amounts upon which such fee is based for calendar years between 2014 and 2018. Imposes a penalty on health insurance providers who understate net premium income subject to such tax.

(Sec. 1407) Delays until 2013 the elimination of the tax deduction for expenses allocable to the Medicare Part D subsidy.

(Sec. 1408) Revises the definition of "cellulosic biofuel" for purposes of the cellulosic biofuel producer tax credit to exclude any fuel if more than 4% of such fuel is any combination of water and sediment or the ash content of such fuel is more than 1% (determined by weight).

(Sec. 1409) Sets forth rules for the application of the economic substance doctrine to transactions affecting taxpayer liability. Treats a transaction as having economic substance if: (1) the transaction changes in a meaningful way the taxpayer's economic position; and (2) the taxpayer has a substantial purpose, other than tax avoidance, for entering into a transaction. Imposes penalties for underpayments attributable to transactions lacking economic substance.

(Sec. 1410) Increases by 15.75% in the third quarter of 2014, the estimated tax payment of corporations with assets of $1 billion or more.

Subtitle F: Other Provisions

(Sec. 1501) Amends the Trade Act of 1974 to make appropriations for the community college and career training grant program for FY2011-FY2014. Requires that states receive not less than .5% of amounts appropriated in each fiscal year.

Title II: Education and Health

Subtitle A: Education—SAFRA Act

Part I: Investing in Students and Families

(Sec. 2101) Amends the Higher Education Act of 1965 to authorize and appropriate such sums as may be necessary to fully fund maximum Pell Grant amounts, beginning in FY2010. Authorizes and appropriates an additional amount for FY2011.

Establishes a new formula for determining increases in the maximum Pell Grant award beginning with the 2013-2014 school year.

Ties increases in the maximum Pell Grant amount, from the 2013-2014 school year through the 2017-2018 school year, to increases in the Consumer Price Index.

(Sec. 2102) Authorizes and appropriates funds for the College Access Challenge Grant program for FY2010-FY2014. Terminates the authority of the Secretary of Education (Secretary, for purposes of this subtitle) to award grants under such program after FY2014.

Increases the minimum state allotment under such program from 0.5% to 1% of the total amount appropriated for such program in a fiscal year.

(Sec. 2103) Extends funding for grants to historically Black colleges and universities and other minority-serving institutions through FY2019. Terminates the Secretary's authority to award such grants after FY2019.

Part II: Student Loan Reform

(Sec. 2201) Prohibits any new loans from being made or insured under the Federal Family Education Loan (FFEL) program after June 2010, including payments to reduce student costs and FFEL Plus Loans.

(Sec. 2206) Allows borrowers who have loans under both the Direct Loan (DL) and FFEL programs, or who have a loan under either program as well as an FFEL that has been sold to the Secretary, to consolidate such loans under the DL program from July 2010 through June 2011, if the borrower has not begun repaying such loans.

(Sec. 2207) Terminates after June 2010 unsubsidized Stafford Loans for middle-income borrowers and special allowances.

(Sec. 2209) Requires DLs for students and the parents of students attending institutions of higher education (IHEs) outside of the United States to be disbursed through a financial institution located or operating in the United States which is designated by the Secretary to receive DL funds and transfer them to such schools.

(Sec. 2212) Directs the Secretary to: (1) award DL servicing contracts to nonprofit servicers that meet certain federal standards and have the capacity to service their loan account allocation; (2) allocate the loan accounts of 100,000 borrowers to each of the nonprofit servicers; and (3) establish a separate pricing tier for each of the first 100,000 borrower loan accounts at a competitive market rate.

Permits the Secretary to reallocate, increase, reduce, or terminate a nonprofit servicer's allocation based on the performance of such servicer.

Makes nonprofit servicers ineligible for such contracts if they have not been awarded such a contract before July 1, 2014, or have had their contract terminated and not been awarded a new contract before such date.

Provides funding to the Secretary, from FY2010-2019, for the administrative costs of servicing such contracts.

Directs the Secretary to provide IHEs with technical assistance in establishing and administering DL programs. Authorizes and appropriates FY2010 funding for the provision of such assistance.

Requires the Secretary to provide payments to loan servicers for retaining jobs at locations in the United States where such servicers were operating under the FFEL program on January 1, 2010. Authorizes and appropriates FY2010-FY2011 funding for the provision of such payments.

(Sec. 2213) Lowers the cap on annual, income-based student loan repayments for new borrowers after July 1, 2014 from 15% to 10% of the amount by which a borrower's and the borrower's spouse's adjusted gross income exceeds 150% of the poverty line.

Requires the Secretary to forgive the remaining balance of such loans after 20 (currently, 25) years of repayment.

Subtitle B: Health

(Sec. 2301) Amends the Patient Protection and Affordable Care Act (PPACA) to apply to grandfathered health plans for plan years beginning on or after January 1, 2014, provisions that prohibit a health plan from applying any waiting period for coverage that exceeds 90 days. (A grandfathered health plan is a group health plan or health insurance coverage in which an individual was enrolled on the date of enactment of PPACA.)

Applies to grandfathered health plans for plan years beginning on or after six months after enactment of PPACA provisions that: (1) prohibit a health plan from establishing lifetime limits on the dollar value of benefits for any participant or beneficiary; (2) prohibit a health plan from rescinding coverage of an enrollee except in the case of fraud or intentional misrepresentation of material fact; and (3) require a health plan that provides dependent coverage of children to make such coverage available for an adult child under 26 years of age.

Applies to grandfathered group health plans for plan years beginning on or after January 1, 2014, provisions that: (1) prohibit a health plan from establishing annual limits on the dollar value of benefits for any participant or beneficiary, except that restrictions on annual limits apply for plan years beginning on or after six months after enactment of PPACA; and (2) prohibit a health plan from imposing any preexisting condition exclusions, except that such requirements apply for plan years beginning on or after six months after enactment of PPACA for enrollees under 19 years of age.

Requires grandfathered group health plans for plan years beginning before January 1, 2014, to provide dependent coverage to an adult child until age 26 only if such child is not eligible to enroll in an employer-sponsored health plan other than such grandfathered health plan.

Repeals the requirement that an adult child be unmarried in order to qualify for dependent coverage until age 26.

(Sec. 2302) Limits the 340B drug discount program to outpatient drugs and removes exceptions to the prohibition on enrolled hospitals obtaining covered outpatient drugs through a group purchasing organization or a group purchasing arrangement (thus restoring the provisions in effect before enactment of PPACA). Excludes certain drugs designated for a rare disease or condition as covered outpatient drugs for covered entities added to the program under PPACA.

(Sec. 2303) Increases the authorization of appropriations for FY2011-FY2015 to the Community Health Center Fund to provide enhanced funding for the community health center program.

Index

ACA. *See* Affordable Care Act of 2010 (ACA)

Accountable care organizations (ACOs), 52, 61–63, 68; joint ventures for, 98–99; local, 96, 98; Medicaid, 82; Medicare, 62, 63–64, 97, 98; physicians' engagement in, 78; as response to healthcare inflation, 80; risk management function of, 115–116; specialty, 96

Action Plan to Prevent Healthcare-Associated Infections, 28

Acute Care Episode (ACE) Demonstration, 63–64, 69

Administration for Children and Families, 31

Administrative costs, 73, 92

Affinity groups, 99

Affordable Care Act of 2010 (ACA), 1. *See also* Funds flow and incentives theory; Markets theory; Health Care and Education Reconciliation Act; Patient Protection and Affordable Care Act; Systems theory: chronic disease management policy of, 10, 17–26, 49–56, 109, 114–115, 137–140; full implementation of, 93; fundamental theories of, 1–2, 3; funding sources for, 108; groundwork for, 2–3; healthcare homes policy of, 21–24, 50, 115; lack of funding for, 104; lawsuits against, 104; prevention and wellness policies of, 37–47; primary care policy of, 10–11, 23–24; productivity and quality improvement policy of, 27–35, 30–31, 33, 109, 115, 129–137; public option of, 107; public programs policy of, 72, 125–129; repeal of, 108–109; sources of policies contained in, 3; strategies for changing, 103–105; Title I, 8, 117–125; Title II, 72, 125–129; Title III, 27–35, 129–137; Title IV, 39, 137–140; Title V, 5, 23–24, 66, 111–112, 140–143; Title VI, 66, 143–149; Title VII, 149; Title VIII, 149–150; Title IX, 149–150; Title X, 151–156

Agency for Healthcare Research and Quality (AHRQ): ACA provision for, 32, 33; clinical decision support role of, 21; involvement in

National Quality Improvement Strategy, 31; support for healthcare reform by, 32

Alaska, rural healthcare in, 74

Alternative care models, 52

American Academy of Family Physicians, 22, 26

American Academy of Pediatrics, 22

American College of Physicians, 22

American Osteopathic Association, 22

American Recovery and Reinvestment Act (ARRA), 19, 25, 26, 42, 49, 109

Associations, involvement in healthcare policy, 110–111

Axolotl system, 81, 84

Bandhold, Hans, 9

Baptist Health system, Texas, 63

Basic research, 5

Baucus, Max, 2–3

Berman, Abe, 111–112

Budgets, global, 78, 107

Bundled payments, 9, 63–64, 78, 80, 108, 115–116

California, Kaiser Permanente healthcare system in, 96

California Healthy Eating, Active Communities Program, 42, 43–45

"Call to Action: Health Reform 2009" report, 2–3

Canada, 107

Capitalism, market-based, 2, 7

Capitation: global, 73; partial, 98

Cardiologists, salaries of, 50

Center for Medicare and Medicaid Innovation (CMI), 67, 73, 108, 111

Centers for Disease Control and Prevention (CDC), 31

Centers for Medicare & Medicaid Services (CMS), 29; accountable care organizations (ACOs) and, 63; involvement in National Quality Improvement Strategy, 31; Medicare Acute Care Episode (ACE) Demonstration

Nebraska, rural healthcare in, 74
Nevada, rural healthcare in, 74
New Mexico, rural healthcare in, 74
New York Times, 62–63
Nixon, Richard M., 111–112
North Dakota, rural healthcare in, 74
Nutrition: public education programs in, 39;
    school-based programs in, 39–40, 42, 43–45

Obama, Barack, 104, 105
Obesity: childhood, 43–45; in children and
    adolescents, 39–40
Office of Management and Budget, 31
Office of the National Coordinator for Health
    Information Technology, 31
Ohio, Kaiser Permanente healthcare system
    in, 96
Oral health, 39
Oregon, Kaiser Permanente healthcare system
    in, 96
Outcomes research, patient-centered, 5,
    20–21, 145
Outreach, in chronic disease management, 17

Partnerships, physician-hospital, 80–81
Patient-centered outcomes research, 5, 20–21, 145
Patient engagement, in shared decision
    making, 24–25
Patient experience, performance evaluation
    of, 60
Patient Protection and Affordable Care Act, 12,
    13; summary of, 117–156
Patient-provider system, 3, 4–5
Pay-for-performance systems, 115
Payment policies. *See also* Incentives, as
    payment system component; Penalties, as
    payment system component: backup plans
    for, 67–68; classification of, 60
Payment systems, global, 73
Penalties, as payment policy component, 60,
    64–67; for hospital-acquired conditions,
    65–66, 108; for unnecessary readmissions,
    64–65, 108
Performance monitoring, in shared decision
    making, 25
Physician Feedback System, 28–29
Physician Group Practice (PGP)
    Demonstration, 62
Physician–hospital relationship, 78
Physician Quality Reporting Initiative (PQRI),
    28–29
Physicians. *See also* Primary care physicians:
    accountable care organizations of, 80;
    financial influences on, 5–6; quality
    evaluation of, 29; salary caps for, 107
Pledge of Allegiance, 87

Population health, 39, 109
Praxel, Theodore A., 63
Preexisting conditions: denial of health
    insurance based on, 41, 88, 105, 108, 119;
    implication for wellness programs,
    40–41, 42
Presidential election (2012), 105
Preventive care, 37–47, 115; clinical prevention
    component of, 37–40; community building
    component of, 37, 41–42; individual
    wellness component of, 37, 40–41; scenarios
    of, 53–55, 56; strategies for, 54–55, 56
Preventive Services Task Force, 39
Primary care. *See also* Primary care physicians:
    ACA provision for, 23–24, 140–143;
    healthcare home concept of, 21–24, 50, 115;
    as health plan service, 99
Primary care physicians: hospital-employed, 52;
    increasing the supply of, 5, 23–24, 50–52,
    108, 115, 140–143; salaries of, 50; specialty
    consultations to, 96
Primary care practices: acquisition by large
    integrated providers, 97; acquisition by
    national health plans, 97; health
    information technology (HIT) use in, 39
Productivity, 27–30; improvement of, 29–30;
    value-based purchasing and, 27–29
Prospective payment system, DRG-based, 6–7,
    28–29, 74
Pseudomonas aeruginosa infections, 65
Public education, regarding preventive services,
    39–40
Public health, 39
Public health agencies, prevention and wellness
    programs of, 55
Public health departments, prevention and
    wellness programs of, 38
Public option, 107
Purchasing, value-based, 27–29, 30, 78

Quality, of healthcare: ACA provisions for,
    30–32, 33, 129–137; clinical, 60; versus
    maximized revenue and profit, 6;
    unevenness of, 27
Quality reporting, 30–31, 33, 109, 115; improved
    systems for, 60; state-based agencies for, 60

RAND, 88
Rationing, of healthcare, 60
Readmissions, prevention of, 64–65, 68
Recovery Audit Contractors (RAC) program,
    66–67, 68
Resources, markets model of, 8
Restaurants, nutritional postings in, 39
Retail-branded healthcare, 97–98
Retail clinics, 52, 54–55

Risk-pool death spiral, 105
Rural healthcare, 73–74, 81

Safety, of healthcare: performance evaluation
   of, 60; unevenness of, 27
Safety-net healthcare providers, 71–76, 116;
   CHIP eligibility and, 81; community clinics,
   74–75, 81; community engagement of, 81–83,
   84; for dual Medicare/Medicaid beneficiaries,
   72–73; Medicaid eligibility and, 81–83, 84;
   public hospitals, 73, 81; of rural healthcare,
   73–74, 81; scenarios, 81–83, 84
Safeway, 40, 47
St. Vincent's Hospital, New York City, 82
Salaries, of physicians, 56; caps on, 107; for
   specialists, 115
Scenarios and scenario planning, 9–11, 12; basic
   goals in, 10; for chronic disease
   management, 49–52; for consumer
   engagement, 53–55, 56; for funds flow,
   77–84; for markets (health insurance
   coverage), 95–100; for prevention and
   wellness programs, 53–55, 56; for systems
   theory, 49–56
School-based clinics, 39–40
School-based wellness programs, 42, 43–45
Shadow pricing, 91
Shared savings concept, 61
Social Security Administration, 31
South Dakota, rural healthcare in, 74
Specialists: consultations with, 96; independent
   practices of, 78; salaries of, 115
Specialty accountable care organizations
   (ACOs), 96
Staphylococcus aureus, methicillin-resistant
   (MRSA), 65
State health insurance exchanges, 108
States. *See also specific states:* "frontier," 74;
   healthcare inflation rates in, 109; lawsuits
   against ACA from, 104
Substance Abuse and Mental Health Services
   Administration, 31
Surgical Care Improvement Project (SCIP),
   28, 34
Systems theory, of the ACA, 1, 2, 3–5, 12, 109; of
   chronic disease management, 17–26; of
   healthcare productivity and quality, 27–35;
   of prevention and wellness, 37–47; scenarios
   of, 49–56

Target stores, 51, 54
Taxes, ACA-mandated, 106

Tourism, medical, 97–98

Uncompensated care. *See also* Uninsured
   populations: reduction in, 6
Uninsured populations: chronic disease
   management in, 88, 89; pediatric, 72; safety-
   net healthcare for, 71–76
UnitedHealth Group, 40, 81, 84
United States Congress, oversight hearings
   by, 104
United States Constitution, commerce clause
   of, 104
United States Department Commerce, 31
United States Department of Defense, 31
United States Department of Health and
   Human Services, 40; accountable care
   organizations regulations of, 61, 62; Action
   Plan to Prevent Healthcare-Associated
   Infections, 28; health insurance benefits
   determination by, 90–91; involvement
   in National Quality Improvement
   Strategy, 31
United States Department of Labor, 31
United States Department of Veterans Affairs, 31
United States Hospital Referral Regions, 24
United States Office of Personnel
   Management, 31
United States Preventive Services Task Force,
   46–47
Universal health insurance coverage, 87, 88
University of St. Thomas, Center for Health
   and Medical Affairs, 11
Urgent care, 99
Utah, rural healthcare in, 74
Utah Health Exchange, 108

Value-based purchasing, 27–29, 30, 78, 115
Vendors, "value solutions" of, 79
Veterans Health Administration, 31

Wagner, Edward, 17, 19
WalMart, 51, 54
Washington, DC, Kaiser Permanente
   integrated healthcare system in, 96
Washington state, Kaiser Permanente
   integrated healthcare system in, 96
Wellness programs, 40–41, 46, 115; scenarios of,
   53–55, 56; in schools, 39–40; strategies for,
   54–55, 56
WellPoint, 92
Wisconsin, Mayo Health System in, 96
Wyoming, rural healthcare in, 74

About the Author

Daniel McLaughlin, MHA, is director of the Center for Health and Medical Affairs in the Opus College of Business at the University of St. Thomas. Prior to this position, he was executive director of the National Institute of Health Policy at the University of St. Thomas. From 1984 to 1992, Mr. McLaughlin was CEO of Hennepin County Medical Center and director of the county health system.

Mr. McLaughlin has served as chair of the National Association of Public Hospitals and Health Systems. He served on President Clinton's Task Force on Health Care Reform in 1993. He holds degrees in electrical engineering and healthcare administration from the University of Minnesota. In addition to his administrative responsibilities, Mr. McLaughlin is active in teaching and research at the University of St. Thomas, with emphasis on healthcare operations, leadership, and policy.

He is also the author of *Healthcare Operations Management* and *Make It Happen: Effective Execution in Healthcare Leadership.*